THE PA

WILD
FOOD

EDIBLE PLANTS &
RECIPES *for* CANADA

Sandra Walker

Lone Pine Publishing

Distributed by: Canada Book Distributors - Booklogic
11414-119 Street
Edmonton, AB T5G 2X6
Canada
Tel: 1-800-661-9017

Library and Archives Canada Cataloguing in Publication

Walker, Sandra, 1961–, author
    The path to wild food : edible plants & recipes for Canada / Sandra Walker.

Includes bibliographical references and index.
ISBN 978-1-55105-966-2 (softcover) 978-1-55105-967-9 (e-pub)

    1. Wild plants, Edible–Prairie Provinces–Identification.
2. Cooking (Wild foods). 3. Cookbooks. I. Title.

QK98.5.C3W34 2018   581.6'3209712   C2017-908047-4

All Illustrations: Sandra Walker

Photos: All photos are by Ron Heinrichs except: Amanda Dionne, 179; Wade Falk, 26, 64, 75, 159, 180; *Flickr:* Ed Ogle, 109; *Thinkstock:* AGEphotography, 182; alder7, 174; AlekseySagitov, 77; Alexandrum79, 177; AndreaPapaleo, 138; AnnaVolotkovska, 36; ArgenLant, 178; AVTG, 11; bkkm, 154; BONDART, 1; BrianLasenby, 104; brizmaker, 7; CarterPower, 181; Digoarpi, 148; Dimijana, 74; ErikAgar, 45; fedsax, 94, 156; GeorgiosArt, 107; gojak, 35; hkuchera, 87; Ian_Redding, 122; Icealien, 9; jaanalisette, 8; Jeanne Emmel, 171; JinzhaBloodrose, 40; Kamadie, 179; Kati Finell, 167; karayuschij, 23; kazoka30, 109; kbycphotography, 105; LAByrne, 155; Medioimages/Photodisc, 4; MelodyanneM, 166; MIMOHE, 96; Mr_Twister, 172; Nadanka, 121; Nadezhda_Nesterova, 60; nadyatess, 173; Nordroden, 10; OlyaSolodenko, 168; pcturner71, 176; passion4nature, 140; Prosovych, 41; Radionphoto, 38; rannica, 20; Razvan, 169; seven75, 97, 163, 170; Sitikka, 6; Smileus, 5; TongRo Images Inc, 165; vfoto, 29; xtrekx, 161; yokeetod, 12; Yuriy_Kulik, 25; ZayacSK, 160; *Wikipedia:* 98, 158, 175.

Cover Photograph: BONDART/ Thinkstock

We acknowledge the financial support of the Government of Canada.
Nous reconnaissons l'appui financier du gouvernement du Canada.

Funded by the Government of Canada
Financé par le gouvernement du Canada |

PC: 38

Contents

Preface

Since I was a child I have dreamed of writing a book, and I thought it would be an adventure tale. Well I finally got around to it, and here it is, with a bit of a twist. Food is an adventure, and this book is a walk on the wild side to culinary delights.

I got hooked on the pursuit of wild foods while travelling abroad. I loved visiting the local markets and vendors to see what dishes were cooking and to try and decipher the ingredients that went into them, through smell, taste and conversation. Memorable gastronomic events include flying fish, fresh guava and mammee apple. The meals were prepared in unique ways, usually with a reverence for tradition, and were accompanied with regional herbs and spices. I recall one occasion when the dish being served was iguana, a local treat that seemed to bring the community together. No, it didn't taste like chicken, but it was quite tasty and was akin to a spicy pork tenderloin (Hey, you never know until you try!).

My travelling days came to halt for a time when I came back to Canada and had children, but I continued to shop in the exotic markets as much as possible. It soon dawned on me that I had not experienced much of our North American Indigenous cuisine. I searched libraries and bookstores, but literature on Indigenous foods seemed hard to come by.

As I continued my quest for knowledge on this subject, I came across Adam Szczawinski and Nancy Turner's *Wild Green Vegetables of Canada*, and *Edible Garden Weeds of Canada*. Fascinated by their unique recipes and thorough treatment of the subject, I soon collected almost every book they had written. I must admit that these works influenced some of the following recipes, but I added a splash of personal experience and a dash of regional flavour. Thank you to Nancy Turner and Adam Szczawinski for keeping my adventures in food alive and helping to provide impetus for this book.

Also providing momentum for this book is the idea of "think globally, act locally," and how we can reduce our environmental footprint by considering the health of the planet when making everyday decisions in our communities. Currently there is a growing interest in diets that source food from within a relatively small geographical area. For example, the "100-mile diet," in which people only consume food grown or produced within 100 miles of where they live, is one way to decrease impacts on the environment while supporting local economies. While many people flock to harvest fairs and farmers' markets to obtain locally grown food, gathering foods from the wild is another way to eat locally, and it is highly rewarding and educational. It is even possible to grow many wild plants in your yard or garden, and some might already be thriving there without being noticed. The amount of each plant gathered may be meagre, but the foods are usually high in nutrition and rich in taste. Although the path to wild foods might be one less taken, it just might make a difference.

Thank You: Pandora Theriault, Nikki Simmons, Laura Foley, and my husband, Wade Falk, for their helpful comments and suggestions. I also want to thank my youngest son, Josh, for following in my footsteps with his genuine love for camping, hunting, gathering and ethnobotany.

Introduction

What is Ethnobotany?

The U.S. botanist John William Harshberger first coined the term "ethnobotany" in 1895. Ethnobotany combines the study of cultures (ethno/ethnographer) and the study of plants (botany). Cumulatively, ethnobotany is the study of relationships between peoples and plants, often with a focus on how plants are used by various groups. How cultures come to use plants is influenced largely by environmental factors, such as climate, ecosystem, availability and abundance, as well as by cultural variables, social values and technology. Many early cultures used plants for subsistence, medicinally or to make into tools or art. Domestication of plants by most cultures led to food surpluses and technological advances, arguably creating the foundation for contemporary society.

In my work as an ethnobotanist, a question I often encounter is how did humans first learn which plants are edible and which are not. As trial and error probably played a key role, I like to retort "you try it first!", mocking courtesy over self preservation. People also learned food lessons by observing other omnivores, such as bears or pigs, as they are known to have widely varied diets. These observations were also valuable for interpreting medicinal uses of plants for historical, and eventually, contemporary cultures. Through these kinds of experiences and observations, we have come to understand that while only a minority of plants are edible, many plants have a multitude of other uses.

Rediscovering Our Roots

All the vegetables, fruits and grains commonly consumed these days have their ancestral "roots" as wild plants. Wild plant foods are often more diminutive than their modern counterparts, many of which are modified, hybrid derivations of wild plants made possible by the plasticity of the plant genome. Wild plant foods typically have more vitamins and minerals then domesticated plants, but they may also have more toxins and armour. In this way, wild plants may be better at the art of self-defence than modern plant foods. Many plants, however, may bypass self-defence in order to survive in their own way. Many species evolved to be very colourful and tasty looking, to be attractive to the eye of passing herbivores and omnivores, as if to say, "Eat me." Some species also adapted to being food so the seeds would be consumed and exposed to digestive acids in order to scarify the seeds' protective coating prior to germination. In this way, without any help from us, many plants guaranteed the spread of their seed in fertile soils elsewhere, and also helped mitigate overtaxing local soils. Humankind has capitalized on these and other features of plants, first out of necessity and, more recently, as a core element of our globalized economy.

Several million years ago, our human ancestors were hunter-gatherers and were entirely dependent on wild foods. Hunter-gatherers moved frequently following roaming herds and searching constantly for wild foods, thereby increasing their knowledge of different wild plant species. Although they were in competition with each other for survival, animals and plants created complex symbiotic relationships. The interconnectedness and interdependence of these interactions became increasingly understood and was adopted and/or modified by many Indigenous cultures. As plant life evolved, mankind's ancestral relationship with plants also evolved and changed dramatically.

Today it is widely assumed that agricultural food production, which includes the domestication of plants as crops and animals as livestock, began approximately 11,000 years ago, give or take perhaps more than a few millennia. After years of observing the potential for wild plant species to become farmed crops, early human's transition from hunting and gathering to producing food crops took place relatively rapidly in the Fertile Crescent. This, it is widely believed, created the food production revolution that formed the basis of contemporary civilization.

Whether humans intentionally started growing plants as crops or if cultivation grew out of fortunate coincidence is probably a matter of speculation; however, the cozy relationship between people and plants has always been recognized as central. As for the role of coincidence, archaeological evidence shows that plants started to grow out of human waste piles. Humans inadvertently redistributed plants through the simple process of consuming plants in one place and defecating the detritus and seeds in a different place. Seeds were also transported unintentionally on dirt-encrusted clothing and soiled articles carried by various nomadic groups. As people moved from being hunter-gatherers to becoming farmers and planters, a new symbiotic relationship between humans and plants began, with an increased focus on intention, rather than coincidence.

Speculation aside, one could imagine that our ancestors likely took the first steps in agriculture by exploring a variety of available wild plants and eventually domesticating the ones they found worthy of cultivation. Plant food production occurred at different rates around the world; some cultures developed this independently, whereas others acquired knowledge from observing their neighbours, with many cultures likely finding that routinely harvesting plants resulted in a more plentiful and dependable food supply. Cumulatively, these steps led to the availability of more calories per hectare for humans, and because of this advantage, human populations increased dramatically.

Domestication of wild plants in contemporary agriculture has made sweeping differences in the way we feed ourselves. People no longer have to eat food from local sources. Many of us now consume food produced from great distances on vast commercial farms, requiring huge logistical, transportation and distribution networks. These kinds of changes, in turn, have had substantial impacts on the natural world. For instance, converting natural land to large-scale agriculture has ecological costs, such as the reduction of biodiversity and wildlife habitat, reduction in soil fertility and interference with aquatic habitat, rivers and streams. The disappearance of the majority of native grasslands in the central plains of North America to make way for crop production is a good example. Taming plants has made feeding large populations possible and more convenient, but these developments are not without consequence.

In the race to produce more food, generations of horticultural selection and hybridization have focused on improvement in size and cropping ability rather than nutritional content, which likely results in diminished food value and/or taste in many cases. Anyone tasting large strawberries from the store versus small native strawberries from a natural field can attest to this. Modern food sciences have yet to create any new major foods and are only able to manufacture hybridized reproductions of already existing plants. A notable drawback of hybridization is potential loss of genetic diversity of the indigenous plant sources, which otherwise contain inherent resistance to local pathogens and adaptability to climate extremes. Further, as we have become increasingly dependent on modern agriculture, most of us have simply lost the art of being able to feed ourselves without heading to the supermarket.

Reflecting on the path we have taken, it is comforting to know that wild foods are still around us. For those of you who wish to rekindle an interest in wild foods, and to grow an appreciation of the adventure, flavours and intangibles you'll find along the way, read on.

WILDCRAFTING

Ethics and Hazards of Wildcrafting

The practice of harvesting uncultivated plants from "the wild" for food or to be used in medicines is called "wildcrafting." To be sure your wildcrafting is safe and sustainable, there are a few things you should keep in mind.

Before you begin harvesting wild plants, get to know the plants in your area of interest; consult local guidebooks and plant experts, if necessary. Check the status of your target plants to see if they are rare or not; this may vary from province to province. Some species may even be protected in certain areas. You can usually find this information online through provincial Conservation Data Centres or similar institutions, which provide a list of relative abundance and rarity of species.

Also keep in mind that some plants are poisonous. Some plants produce poison when young and others become poisonous as they mature. Also, one part of a plant may be edible, but the rest of the plant may not be.

Getting permission to access land is also a must. Not only does this show respect for private property, it also provides an opportunity to speak to landowners, who may be storehouses of local knowledge and have helpful hints.

When harvesting, take only what you can readily use, and always leave enough plants in situ so they can reproduce themselves. Try to leave behind seeds and/or propagules for future generations. Protect the surrounding habitat: access the area by foot, backfill any holes you dig and do not litter.

You can also try growing wild foods at home, but again, consult local guidebooks to be sure you correctly identify plants and follow any applicable weed regulations. Sometimes the pretty plant by the creek can turn out to be a nasty invasive species that should be controlled where it is and not transported elsewhere.

Getting Ready for the Trail and its Hazards

As most of us know, being out in nature has many potential hazards, such as insect bites, sun exposure and a rash from poison ivy and stinging nettle. While store-bought remedies may be handy, you do not always need them when you are on the trail. When on the path for wild food, many wild plants can be used for remedies, and they are probably closer than a pharmacy or corner store. The following common plants are either hazards or are useful for remedies or have surprising practical utility.

Pasture Sage

Artemisia frigida

Pasture sage grows in fields and pastures across the prairies.
The plant is a perennial with a taproot that forms a crown with
several stems. The leaves are fringed with a silver greenish hue
with fine hairs and are divided into linear segments up the
stem. Flowers are greenish to yellow and form upward on
the branches into clusters.

Medicine
Tea made from the plant was used to reduce fever, as
a gargle for sore throats and as an aroma for headache
relief.

Other
This aromatic herb can be used as an insect repellent
by rubbing it directly on the skin or smouldering it
in a smudge.

Yarrow leaf

Yarrow

Achillea millefolium

This plant is present in many habitats and is frequently found in grasslands and open forests in temperate regions. This perennial spreads mostly from rhizomes and grows 30 to 70 cm (12 to 28") in height. Yarrow flowers grow in small bunches of pink or white clusters. The feathery leaves are similar in appearance to chipmunk tails.

Food
Dry yarrow leaves can be made into tea.

Medicine
Compress the leaves into a paste and use it on insect bites to relieve itching, or make a cold tea from the leaves to soothe the pain of sunburns or minor cuts. The plant has a wide variety of other medicinal uses, too. The leaves can be boiled into a poultice and used on infections as an antibacterial. In Ancient Greece, yarrow was used to stop wounds from bleeding. The plant contains alkaloids, which help reduce clotting time for wounds. Indigenous peoples have used yarrow to help relieve the discomfort of menstrual cramps. Ointment made from the roots along with other plants has been used as a topical rub for sore muscles and bones. The leaves can be chewed to help relieve the pain of toothaches.

Red osier dogwood in flower

Red Osier Dogwood

Cornus sericea

This shrub grows to about 1 to 2 m (3 to 7') in height and prefers moist areas. In June it produces a white to greenish-hued flower cluster. The fruit is a waxy white, and the bark has a reddish colour, hence the name of the plant. The leaves are lance shaped and opposite to one another, with veins that run parallel from the central vein.

Food

The small pit in the fruit has an edible nut, and the berries can be cooked in sweet-and-sour dishes, soups and stews.

Medicine

The bark can be used as a tea for digestive problems. The inner bark contains salicylate, which provides relief for inflammation. Tea made from the bark was used as a wash. The leaves can be chewed into a paste and used as a poultice on insect bites, which soothes pain and reduces swelling almost instantly when applied. It does not taste good, but your saliva is part of the medicine. Try it once and you will remember it for the next time you have an insect bite. The first time I tried a dogwood poultice was with my son, who swells quite a lot when bitten by wasps. During our walk, being the good mother I am, I left the antihistamines in the car, which was parked more than a kilometre away, so we tried the dogwood after an unexpected bite. By the time we got back to the car 15 minutes later, the swelling was gone. About a week later, he was bitten again in the arm in our yard. This time I used an antihistamine, and it took four days for the swelling to go down. We now have a dogwood bush growing in our yard.

Other Uses
Young branches were used for arrow shafts and woven into baskets. The stem pith was hollowed out and used for pipe stems and to make beads.

Dogwood in flower

Snowberry fruit

Snowberry

Syphoricarpos spp.

These short shrubs reach 50 cm to 1 m (20" to 3') in height and are often found growing in patches in grassland depressions, ravines, open wooded areas and over-grazed pastures. The leaves are oval and opposite of each other, and the flowers are bell-shaped and light pink to white. The fruit of the snowberry is light green to purple or white and is waxy looking.

Two species of snowberry are commonly found on the Prairies, including common snowberry *(S. albus)*, with white berries, and western snowberry *(S. occidentalis)*, with light green berries that turn dark purple. Both of these species contain toxins, and the common snowberry is considered poisonous, especially for children; however, if used carefully, each species can be used medicinally.

Medicine

Indigenous peoples have used snowberries as a decongestant and for the treatment of sinus and head colds. A typical dose is 4 to 5 berries, eaten raw. I have tried this remedy using western snowberry, and it worked for me. I swallowed them whole, much like you would a pill, and within 20 minutes my sinuses cleared, my ears

Western snowberry in flower

popped and I could hear better. A colleague of mine had a bad cold and asked if I knew of any plant that could help. I mentioned the snowberries, but I forgot to tell her I swallowed them whole. She chewed them and said her mouth went numb and it hurt to swallow them, but in about 5 minutes she experienced relief similar to what I had experienced.

When made into a tea, snowberries can be used as an eyewash for sore eyes and snow blindness, and can be used to soothe minor cuts and rashes.

To relieve irritation caused by poison ivy, crush the berries into a pasty substance and apply it to the affected area. A co-worker of mine has significant issues with poison ivy, so I told her about the healing properties of snowberries. She decided to give them a try and discovered they worked better than anything she had used before. She was so impressed she asked me if the berries could be frozen without damage so she could use them the next summer, as poison ivy would be in season before she could obtain fresh snowberries. Using frozen snowberries in this fashion was later confirmed to be effective.

Plantain

Plantago spp.

This plant grows on road-
sides and in meadows,
fields, wastelands and
ditches. The plantain
genus contains about
200 species. Common
plantain *(P. major)* is an
introduced perennial plant
that grows 3 to 30 cm
(1 1/4 to 12") in height
and consists of a low
rosette *of* basal leaves
from which one or more
flowering stalks or spikes
develop. Basal leaves are
oval in shape with about
5 parallel veins and
smooth margins. Many
small flowers are densely
distributed along the spike.

Common plantain

Each flower consists of 4 green sepals, a pistil with a single white style, 4 stamens
with pale purple anthers, and a papery corolla with 4 spreading lobes. The flowers
are replaced by ovoid seed capsules
that are individually about 3 mm
(1/8") long at maturity; they are ini-
tially green but become purple or
brown.

Food

Young plantain leaves are high in
vitamins A, C and K and are good in
salads. In India, the seeds are cultivated and ground into a type of flour
known as Indian wheat. Canaries
love plantain seed, and the seeds are
sometimes used in commercial bird
feed.

Medicine

Plantain was traditionally used to treat skin disorders, such as ulcers, bruises, rashes, boils and cuts. The main active substance is the glycoside aucubin, along with mucilage, vitamin C, tannins, citric acid and certain enzymes. Plaintains, including common and narrowleaf plantain *(P. lanceolata)*, is useful as a bactericide and as an anti-inflammatory in ointments or by warming the leaves enough to wilt them and applying them directly to the affected area of skin. Leaf extracts, made by pureeing the leaves with cold water in a blender and then pouring the mixture though a strainer, can be used to promote the healing of wounds and can be applied to insect bites and minor burns. The leaves can be chewed into a paste and used on minor cuts, rashes or skin infections. The plantain extract, when made into a tea, may be used as an expectorant for coughs and inflammatory diseases of the respiratory system. The seed is used in commercial laxatives.

Plantain Ointment

This ointment can be used to treat itching, skin rashes and insect bites

1 cup (250 mL) chopped plantain leaves
Glycerine (enough to cover leaves)

Crush or grind chopped plantain leaves into a paste. Coat leaves with glycerine, place in a dark bottle and shake well. Let mixture stand for 2 weeks before using. Stored in the refrigerator, it will last for several months.

Aspen

Populus tremuloides

Also called: trembling aspen, poplar

Aspen is a circumpolar, deciduous tree that is often medium to small sized but can reach about 20 to 30 m (65 to 100') in height. Often found in bluffs in slight depressions, moist coolies, sheltered spots and riparian areas, aspen is the most common tree in North America. Its greenish-white bark produces rough-ened dark patches around the branches. The leaves are oval to circular with slightly toothed edges. The petiole is flattened, which causes the leaves to "tremble" in the wind.

This tree reproduces through both seed and root. The seeds have a very short window for germination and must sprout within a few days or so after dispersal or they die. The trees make up for this weakness by producing many seeds early in the spring when moisture conditions are good. Aspens also repro-duce by roots and suckering clones. Many aspen bluffs consist of clones with common roots originating from a single tree.

Trembling aspen in spring

Food

The inner bark is sweet and high in vitamin C; many Indigenous peoples have relished it as a treat. Many people in Europe survived food scarcity dur-ing the World Wars by eating the inner bark of these trees. Young aspens are also useful as supplemental animal fodder, and large herbivores, including horses and moose, prefer the young

21

shoots and leaves of this tree. Tapping the trees produces syrup, and boiling the early buds makes a good tea. Indigenous peoples have used the ash from aspen as baking powder. The white power from the bark has been used as an all-purpose baking yeast.

Medicine
Leaf buds have been used to make cough syrups to treat whooping cough, and as a part of a lineament for sore muscles.

Other Uses
When young, the buds are sticky and can be used as an aromatic in a smudge. They are also used as additives in commercial perfumes. The wood burns well when cured and does not snap or pop excessively or make much smoke. The rotten and dry wood was used to smoke meats.

Forgot your sunscreen? An alternative is probably not far away. The bark of the trembling aspen produces a thin layer of white powder that can be used as sunscreen. Simply rub the tree trunk to gather the powder and then rub it directly on exposed skin. Do not overwork the powder or try to rub it into the skin.

As an environmental scientist, my husband works in the field much of the time. He also sunburns very easily, especially at the beginning of spring. One day in May he came home looking as red as a lobster, declaring he had forgotten his sunscreen. I reminded him of the aspen sunscreen and asked him if any trembling aspen grew near where he was working. At that moment, he managed to turn a little redder in the face, and he never came home sunburnt like that again. He has since remarked that, though it is not as effective as high-end commercial sunscreen, even a little of the powder makes a difference.

White powder from the bark of trembling aspen

Stinging Nettle

Potential Plant Hazards

Stinging Nettle
Urtica dioica

This plant, commonly found in moist areas and meadows, has tiny hairs that grow on the leaf and steams; when touched or brushed against, it will often cause an itchy, uncomfortable rash. See the stinging nettle account (p. 125) for more information about this plant.

Dock
Rumex spp.

This weedy perennial plant, often found in moist and disturbed places, can be used as a cure for stinging nettle; rub the leaf juices on the area touched by the stinging nettle to take away the itch and burning sensation. See the dock account (p. 84) for more information about this plant.

Dock

Poison Ivy

Rhus radicans

This plant grows in moist wooded areas in the understory. Poison ivy is a low grow-ing shrub or woody vine. The dark green, waxy leaves are in groups of 3 ("leaves of 3, leave me be"). Leaves are oval leading to a point and are toothed along the edge. The leaf clusters are often drooping. The flowers grow in small white clusters. The fruit is a cluster of whitish berries with light green or gray stripes running longitudi-nally from the stem to the top of the berry.

DO NOT TOUCH. Skin rash will result. The oil on the leaves causes an itchy, irritating rash for most people. All parts of the plant are a potential irritant, even the pollen.

Medicine

Apparently applying the sap from the woody stem directly on a wart can kill the wart virus. No one has been willing to be my tester to try out this treatment.

Trees and Shrubs of the Parkland and Prairie

Many of us know at least a few woody plants in the parkland and prairie that provide a bit of tasty seasonal sustenance, such as saskatoon berries, gooseberries or chokecherries. Many of us have also tried saskatoon berry pie and perhaps rosehip tea—but probably not bearberry dumplings or chokecherry soup. Nor do most of us know that you can use a local birch tree to make beer, or make a fish hook from a hawthorn spine. Of any major plant group, woody plants of the parklands and prairie are among the most productive sources of foods, tools and medicines in the region.

Beaked Hazelnut

Corylus cornuta

This deciduous shrub usually reaches about 3 m (10') in height, growing in moist, well-drained thickets, dry woodlands or forest edges. It has a greyish-brown bark that is fuzzy when young, and broadly oval, fuzzy, toothed leaves. The plant has male and female flowers separated on the same shrub. The male flowers consist of long slender catkins, and the female catkins have tiny, protruding red stigmas. The fruit ripens in autumn, the nuts often forming in fuzzy clusters of 3, with a greenish leafy sheath growing over the shells.

On a camping trip to Good Spirit Lake, north of Yorkton, Saskatchewan, I encountered a thick patch of beaked hazelnut shrubs. Having never picked them before, I gathered a small shopping bag's worth. I soon found I was somewhat allergic to the fine fuzzy hairs on the leaves and husks. I did wear leather gloves, but the fine hairs still made their way through. After husking and shelling the bag of nuts, I ended up with a 1 cup (250 mL) of hazelnuts and used them to make small traditional hazelnut cakes. The cakes (which resemble biscuits) were good and unique tasting, but after all that work and skin irritation, they should have been the best thing I ever ate. Well, at least I can say I have made beaked hazelnut cakes the old fashioned way. And having said that, I would recommend buying a sack of hazelnuts, also called filberts, at the store instead. Apparently Indigenous peoples would sometimes gather the hazelnuts by taking squirrels' stashes of the nuts. I can understand this approach after my experience.

The nuts are small and do not take long to roast in the oven: 10 to 15 minutes at 350°F (175°C) is all it usually takes. I overcooked my first batch, but they had a roasted coffee flavour, so I added them to my coffee grounds and made a rich, nutty tasting coffee.

Food

Indigenous peoples traditionally used hazelnuts for trade goods as well as for food. Hazelnuts were ground into a powder and blended with ground corn, berries or bulbs, then formed into cakes. The mixture was then boiled or fried.

Medicine

Tea from the bark has been used for colds and fevers and as a wash for hives.

Other Uses

The young shoots were used for making arrow shafts and baskets, and the buds, roots and inner bark were used to make a blue dye. Europeans used the shrub to construct wicker fences and to fasten reeds on thatched roofs.

Hazelnuts in hulls

Hazelnut Cakes

Hazelnut Cakes

These cakes are good with maple syrup or jam.

2 cups (500 mL) unroasted, shelled
   hazelnuts
2 cups (500 mL) water
1/3 cup (75 mL) of cornmeal
1/8 tsp. (0.5 mL) salt
1/4 cup (60 mL) cooking oil

Grind nuts in a food processor into
a flour-like consistency. Combine hazelnut flour and water in a medium saucepan and bring to a boil. Reduce heat
and simmer for 30 minutes, stirring frequently. Add cornmeal and salt and let
stand for about 20 minutes, until mixture
thickens into a batter. Heat oil in a frying
pan on medium. Using a spoon, carefully drop dollops of batter into hot oil,
flattening mixture slightly. Cook until
golden brown. Serve hot or cold. Makes
about 25 cakes.

Hazelnut Soup

This recipe makes a rich soup, so small servings are suggested.

1 tsp. (5 mL) cooking oil
1 medium onion, diced
2 cups (500 mL) ground unroasted,
   shelled hazelnuts
4 cups (1 L) beef or chicken stock
1/2 tbsp. (7 mL) parsley
Salt, to taste
Pepper, to taste

Heat oil in a medium frying pan over
medium. Add onion and cook, stirring
occasionally, until onion is caramelized,
about 30 minutes. Combine remaining
ingredients in a medium pot. Add onions
and bring to a boil. Simmer for about
30 minutes, stirring occasionally. Makes
6 servings.

Butter-Toasted Hazelnuts

3 cups (750 mL) shelled hazelnuts
1 tbsp. (15 mL) unsalted butter
1/4 tsp. (1 mL) finely ground sea salt
1 tbsp. (15 mL) fresh thyme leaves
Zest of 1/2 orange
Zest of 1 lemon

Place hazelnuts in a single layer on
a rimmed baking sheet. Toast nuts in
350°F (175°C) oven for about 10 to
15 minutes, until they become fragrant
and skins darken and begin to split.
Remove from oven and set aside. Melt
butter in a large skillet over medium for
about 1 minute. Grind nuts in a blender.
Add to melted butter. Stir in remaining
4 ingredients. Remove from heat and let
stand until cool. Store in refrigerator for
up to 8 weeks. Makes 3 cups (750 mL).

Chicken Scaloppini with Hazelnut Cream Sauce

2 boneless, skinless chicken breast
   halves
Pepper, to taste
1 tbsp. (15 mL) butter
1 tbsp. (15 mL) canola oil
1 large shallot, minced (about 1/4 cup,
   60 mL)
1/4 cup (60 mL) Madeira wine
1/3 cup (75 mL) heavy whipping cream
1/4 cup (60 mL) hazelnuts, toasted and
   chopped

Place chicken between 2 pieces of
waxed paper or plastic wrap. Using
a mallet, pound to about 1/3 inch (1 cm)
thick. Sprinkle pepper on both sides.
Heat butter and oil in a heavy large frying
pan over medium heat. Add chicken and
cook until lightly browned and cooked
through, about 1 to 2 minutes per side.
Transfer chicken to a plate and cover to
keep warm. Set aside.

Add shallot to same frying pan and cook
until tender, about 3 minutes. Pour in
Madeira and bring to boil, stirring to
scrape up and incorporate any browned
bits. Add cream and bring to a boil until
sauce thickens slightly, about 2 minutes.
Stir in hazelnuts. Pour sauce over
chicken and serve. Makes 2 servings.

Hazelnut Vinaigrette

1/2 cup (125 mL) rice vinegar
1/2 cup (125 mL) hazelnut oil
1 cup (250 mL) sunflower oil
1 tbsp. (15 mL) lime juice
1 tbsp. (15 mL) lemon juice

Combine all ingredients in a bottle with
a tight fitting, locking lid. Shake vigorously until well combined. Store in
refrigerator for 3 months. Makes 2 cups
(500 mL).

Paper Birch

Betula papyrifera
var. *papyrifera*

Paper birch is a deciduous tree growing from 15 to 30 m (50 to 100') in height. The tree usually grows in open to dense woodland with moist soils. The bark is white and smooth with scattered grey rough spots. It peels like paper. The leaves have a diamond shape with small, toothed points. Both male and female flowers are on the same tree and form dense, slender clusters called catkins.

Food

In spring the sap is thin and watery and can be used as a refreshment; it can also be boiled down like sugar maple sap, but it does not thicken as much. It takes about 360 to 450 L (80 to 100 gal) of birch sap to make 4.5 L (1 gal) of birch syrup, which is about double the amount of sap needed to make 4.5 L (1 gal) of sugar maple syrup. The sap is reduced to syrup by boiling off nearly all the water, leaving only the sugars and other nutrients naturally found in the birch sap.

Young twigs, seedpods and inner bark can be boiled for tea.

Medicine

Currently research on the birch is ongoing as a treatment for skin cancers.

Other Uses

Birch bark is good for starting fires, and cured wood is hard and burns long. Old or rotten birch wood creates an aromatic smoke that has been used for curing meats.

Nomadic tribes developed birch-bark biting into an art form and created bark baskets, which were lightweight and held water well. Eastern birch trees were often used to construct snowshoes and canoes and are still used in furniture making today.

River Birch

Betula occidentalis

This species grows near creeks or on riverbanks in moist soils in sheltered areas, as well as in low, moist areas in sandhills. This deciduous, smallish tree or shrub usually grows in clusters, often from 5 to 10 m (16 to 33') in height. The smooth bark has scattered brown rough spots and has a purplish-brown to reddish colour. Similar to paper birch, the bark also peels off like paper, although not as readily. Leaves have a diamond shape with small-toothed points. Both male and female flowers are on the same tree forming dense, slender catkins.

Food

Similar to paper birch, the sap can be boiled down. It can be used for syrups, vinegars, beer and even birch wine, or simply kept cool for a refreshing drink. Boil the young twigs, seedpods and inner bark for tea. Tree sap spoils quickly, so it is best to collect the sap in small batches and to filter and process it as soon as possible. Also, keep your collecting bucket covered and protected from rain and bugs.

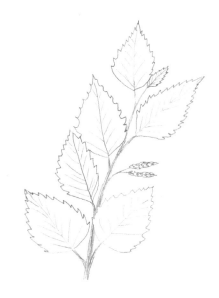

Birch Beer

My husband, Wade Falk, tried this recipe, adapting from Gibbons (1962) and using the sap and twigs from a river birch that was growing in our backyard.

Brewer's yeast or wine yeast can be used in this recipe. Wine yeast will turn out a mead-like product. With brewer's yeast you'll get a carbonated beer-like beverage if it is bottled at the right time.

18 cups (4.5 L) birch sap
4 cups (1 L) honey
1 (.39 oz., 11 g) package wine
** or beer yeast**

Stir honey into sap and bring to a boil for about 10 minutes. Watch the brew, stirring frequently, and adjust temperature to maintain a slight boil. Add a few litres (or more to taste) of finely chopped young birch twigs and let the brew (or wort) cool to room temperature. Strain out the twigs while pouring the brew into a primary fermenting container (a clean bucket with a lid or a covered crock will do). Add yeast and let stand at room temperature away from sunlight and drafts. When the brew has settled and fermentation is complete (usually in about 1 to 2 weeks), you should be ready for the next step. Make sure fermentation is complete before moving to the next step.

If you prefer a carbonated beer-like beverage, bottle the liquid at this time. Depending on your level of experience, you may want to move (or "rack" using a siphon/hose) the beer from the primary container to a carboy, secondary container or bucket before bottling, to minimize sediment introduction into the final product. Preferably after racking, and just before bottling and capping, add a small amount of sugar (about 1 tsp.,

5 mL, per bottle) to the beer. Trace yeast remaining in the liquid will ferment this sugar in the sealed bottles, producing carbon dioxide. This step gives the beer its bubbly fizz. If you are adding sugar at the bottling stage, use bottles that can withstand pressures of carbonation (such as beer bottles), otherwise the bottles may explode. If you don't want carbonation, don't add the sugar, but it is still a good idea to use bottles that can withstand some pressure if the batch is bottled soon after fermentation is considered complete. Let the bottled batch stand in a dark place at room temperature for a few weeks or longer. Cool before serving.

If you've used wine yeast or an aggressive champagne yeast and want a bubbly consistency, treat and bottle the mixture the same as beer. If you prefer a mead-like wine, rack the wine from the primary and into a secondary container or carboy (with an air-lock) and let stand for a month or longer until clear (*no bubbles present in the secondary*) before bottling as a wine. Makes 16 cups (4 L). Fills 12 beer bottles.

If you haven't much brewing experience, check some websites or books for the finer points of brewing, especially as it relates to general process, sterilization and cleanliness.

Immature juniper fruit

Juniper
Juniperus spp.

Juniper typically grows on dry, exposed upland areas with lighter, sandy soil. It is a low-growing shrub typically reaching about 30 cm (1') in height with prostrate, trailing branches. This pioneer shrub helps re-establish disturbed or mobile soil. The greyish-green leaves are lanced and narrow. Juniper berries are biennial, maturing every two years, and are ready when they have a deep blue colour.

Two species of Juniper are commonly found in the Prairies, including creeping juniper *(J. horizontalis)* and the more "upright" low juniper. *(J. communis)*.

Food
When dried and ground, the berries can be used like peppercorns, and tea can be made from the young buds. In Europe, the berries are commonly used on meats and for making corned beef.

33

Medicine

Traditionally green berries were boiled into tea and used to treat kidney issues. The inner bark was soaked to soften it and was used as a poultice on wounds.

Other Uses

Branches were used for bedding to help reduce insect infestations, and the oil was extracted from the berries to make insect repellent.

Trout Stuffed with Juniper and Wild Rice

1/2 cup (125 mL) wild rice
1/2 cup (125 mL) water
1/2 cup (125 mL) orange juice
1/2 cup (125 mL) white rice
1 1/2 tsp. (7 mL) ground juniper berries
1 tsp. (5 mL) ground coriander
Pepper, to taste
1/2 cup (125 mL) of flax seeds
1 medium orange, sliced
1 medium lemon, sliced
1 whole trout (about 4 lbs., 1.8 kg)

Combine wild rice, water and orange juice and cook over medium for about 20 minutes. Add white rice and cook for another 20 minutes, until rice is tender. Stir in next 4 ingredients. Stuff trout with rice mixture and lay orange and lemon slices on top of fish. Wrap fish in aluminum foil or parchment paper and bake in 350°F (175°C) oven for about 45 to 60 minutes, until fish meat flakes off readily with a fork. Makes 2 servings.

Juniper Roasted Cornish Hen

1 1/2 tsp. (7 mL) juniper berries, crushed
Salt, to taste
Pepper, to taste
2 Cornish hens
1/4 cup (60 mL) hazelnut oil

Combine juniper, salt and pepper. Pat hens dry and rub seasoning under skin. Place in a roasting pan and brush skin with hazelnut oil. Cook in 425°F (220°C) oven, basting occasionally with nut oil, for 35 to 40 minutes. Cut hens in half. Makes 4 servings.

Mature juniper fruit

Garlic Potatoes with Juniper Berries

3 tbsp. (45 mL) extra virgin olive oil

2 tbsp. (45 mL) dried juniper berries, crushed

8 large garlic cloves

1 1/2 lbs. (680 g) new potatoes

Juice of 1 small lemon

Coarse-grain sea salt, to taste

Pepper, to taste

1 tbsp. (15 mL) finely chopped fresh oregano

Pour olive oil into a heavy, shallow baking dish, large enough to hold potatoes in a single layer. Sprinkle juniper into oil. Warm dish in 350°F (175°C) oven for a few minutes.

Trim stem ends from garlic cloves and rub off any feathery outer skin. Place potatoes and garlic in warmed dish and stir to coat with oil. Bake, covered, for 10 minutes. Reduce heat to 300°F (150°C). Stir potato mixture and bake uncovered for 50 minutes, until potatoes are just tender. To serve, sprinkle with lemon juice, salt, pepper and oregano. Makes 5 servings.

Juniper Berries with Pork Chops

1/2 lemon

4 pork chops

5 juniper berries, crushed

2 tsp. (10 mL) chopped rosemary

1 tbsp. (15 mL) chopped fresh parsley

Salt, to taste

Pepper, to taste

1 medium green apple

1 tbsp. (15 mL) melted butter

Squeeze lemon juice on both sides of pork chops and season with juniper, rosemary, parsley, salt and pepper. Place chops in a buttered, shallow casserole dish. Core apple, cut into thin slices and place on top of chops. Pour melted butter overtop. Bake in 350°F (175°C) oven for 30 minutes. Makes 4 servings.

Juniper and Wild Plum Sauce

Use this sauce over roasted chicken or any fowl, as well as pork.

2 tbsp. (30 mL) butter
5 wild or green onions
2 garlic cloves
8 crushed juniper berries
2 bay leaves
1/4 cup (60 mL) wild plums, pitted and chopped
4 cups (1 L) chicken stock
2 tsp. (10 mL) tomato paste
Salt, to taste
Pepper, to taste

Melt butter in a saucepan over medium. Add onions and garlic and cook, stirring occasionally, until onions are softened. Add juniper, bay leaves and plums and cook until plums are tender. Set aside to cool and remove bay leaves. Puree cooled mixture in a food processor. In same saucepan, add chicken stock, tomato paste and pureed plum mixture. Season with salt and pepper. Makes 4 1/2 cups (1.1 L).

Black Currant

Ribes nigrum

This low-growing shrub reaches about 90 cm to 1.2 m (3 to 4') in height. It is found in moist soils in the parklands. The stem of a black currant has thorns. The mature bark appears as though it is peeling and has a brownish-grey colour with a yellowish-red colour underneath when exposed. The dark green, maple-leaf-shaped leaves are alternate, and are somewhat hairy. The white, bell-shaped flowers form a grape-like cluster. Flowers appear in late May and early June.

Food

The berries can be eaten raw or cooked in a variety of ways and are used in jams, jellies, sauces, pies, muffins and wine. The flowers are also edible and work nicely in salads. Indigenous peoples often served currant sauces with fish and fish roe (eggs).

Medicine

Indigenous peoples have made a tea of the bark to treat colds and the flu. Currants continue to be recognized for their health benefits and are currently used in cold medicines and throat lozenges.

Black Currant Sauce

This sauce can be served hot or cold. It is great on chicken and pork.

1 tbsp. (15 mL) olive oil
1 small onion, finely chopped
1 tbsp. (15 mL) port
1 1/3 cups (325 mL) chicken stock
1 tbsp. (15 mL) butter
1 tbsp. (15 mL) honey
3/4 cup (175 mL) black currants
1/2 tsp. (2 mL) salt
1 tsp. (5 mL) Pepper

Heat olive oil in a saucepan on medium. Add onion and cook for 2 to 3 minutes, until softened but not browned. Add port and scrape any browned bits from bottom of pan with a wooden spoon. Reduce heat and add chicken stock. Simmer until reduced by half. Whisk in butter and honey until melted. Stir in black currants and crush with a potato masher. Season with salt and pepper. Simmer gently for 2 to 3 minutes. Store in refrigerator for up to 1 week. Makes 1 1/2 cups (375 mL).

Black Currant Orange Salad

This salad is great alone or when served with roasted chicken or ham.

2 cups (500 mL) of fresh black currants
3 mandarin oranges, peeled, skinned and chopped
1/2 cup (125 mL) granulated sugar
1 (3 oz., 85 g) box of raspberry jelly powder (gelatine)
1 cup (250 mL) boiling water
2 cups (500 mL) cold water

Combine currants, oranges and sugar in a bowl and let stand for 2 hours at room temperature. Stir jelly powder into boiling water until dissolved. Pour over fruit and stir, if necessary, to ensure sugar has dissolved. Add cold water and let set in fridge. Makes 4 servings.

Red Currant

Ribes rubrum

Red currant grows in moist soils in the parklands and prairies. This shrub is approximately 1 m (3') in height, with leaves that are maple-leaf shaped and grow alternate to one another. The flowers are reddish purple and oval shaped with 5 petals forming a drooping cluster. Flowers appear in late May and early June.

Food

The berries can be eaten raw or cooked in a variety of ways and are used in jams, jellies, sauces, pies, muffins and wine. The flowers are also edible and work nicely in salads.

Medicinal Uses

Tea from the leaves and berries have been used to treat colds, coughs and sore throats.

Red Currant and Raspberry Jam

3 cups (750 mL) red currants
3/4 cup (175 mL) water
4 cups (1 L) raspberries
6 cups (1.5 L) granulated sugar
1 (2 oz., 57 g) package of pectin crystals

Combine currants and water in a large pot over high heat. Bring to a boil and cook for 10 minutes. Remove from heat and mash berries. Add remaining 3 ingredients and bring back to a boil over low heat. Simmer for about 20 minutes. Pour into sterilized jars. Makes 6 cups (1.5 L).

Wild Gooseberry

Ribes spp.

This low-growing shrub grows to about 1 to 2 m (3 to 7') in height. Belonging to the currant family, wild gooseberry grows in moist woods, stream banks and damp meadows. The leaves are alternate and are similar to maple leaves but are somewhat rounded at the tips. The flowers have 5 petals and are greenish yellow. Gooseberry fruits are one of the first berries to be edible in the early summer and are a bright green that turns purple as they mature. The greenish fruits are quite tart but sweeten as they darken.

Food
The fruits can be eaten fresh from the bush and also make a great jam or jelly.

Medicine
Tea from the leaves and berries has been used to treat colds, coughs and sore throats.

Other Uses
The stems have variegated thorns that have been used as small fish hooks. The root system has a mesh-like quality and can be made into a fishnet when bound together.

Gooseberry Leather

4 cups (1 L) gooseberries
1 cup (250 mL) water
1/2 cup (125 mL) honey

Combine all 3 ingredients in a large pot
and bring to a boil. Reduce heat and simmer for 10 minutes. Pour into a blender, or
use an immersion blender, and puree. Place
wax paper on a cookie sheet and spread puree
out on paper to 6 mm (1/4') thick. Cook in 200°F
(95°C) oven for 4 to 6 hours, until mixture sets and
becomes leathery. Store in a sealed container for up
to 2 weeks. Cuts into 24 pieces.

Bunchberry in flower

Bunchberry

Cornus canadensis

Also called: dwarfed dogwood

A member of the *Cornaceae* or dogwood family, bunchberry is a perennial typically found growing in shady woodlands of boreal forests and parklands. It grows to about 10 to 20 cm (4 to 8") in height, generally forming a carpet-like mat of clone colonies underneath trees. The above-ground shoots rise from slender, creeping rhizomes about 2.5 to 7.5 cm (1 to 3") beneath the soil. Bunchberry leaves grow near the terminal node, are oppositely arranged on the stem, and form a cluster of 4 green leaves. In late spring to midsummer, bunchberry plants produce white flowers with ovate-lanceolate shaped petals.

Food

Bunchberries can be used as an emergency food; however, they are not sweet. They can be combined with other wild berries in pies, jellies, sauces and jams. Bunchberry is high in pectin and helps to thicken stewed fruit or berries.

Medicine

Traditionally berries were made into tea to treat symptoms of heartburn.

Bunchberry Sauce

This sauce is a good complement for pork or turkey and is delicious on ice cream.

4 cups (1 L) bunchberries
1/2 cup (125 mL) fruit punch
1/4 cup (60 mL) granulated sugar
1 tbsp. (15 mL) lemon juice
1 tsp. (5 mL) ground cinnamon
Ground nutmeg, to taste
Ground cardamom, to taste

Combine berries and fruit punch in a medium pot and bring to a boil. Reduce heat and simmer for 10 minutes. Remove from heat, cool mixture somewhat, and then run mixture though a strainer, using a spoon to mush pulp and press liquid through strainer. Discard skins and seeds, and return strained pulp to pot. Add remaining ingredients and simmer until sugar is dissolved. Store in referigerator for 1 week. Makes 4 1/2 cups (1.1 L).

Bunchberry Raspberry Fruit Sauce

Serve this sauce over your favourite pancakes, or use the following crepe recipe.

2 cups (500 mL) bunchberries
2 cups (500 mL) raspberries
1/4 cup (60 mL) mixed fruit juice
1/4 cup (60 mL) honey

Place fruit in a small saucepan with fruit juice and honey. Bring to a boil and cook until the fruit is soft, about 10 minutes. Remove from heat and let cool somewhat. Pour mixture through a colander, pressing cooked fruit with a spoon. Store strained mixture in a sealed jar in refrigerator for 3 to 4 weeks. Makes 4 1/2 cups (1.1 L).

Basic Crepes with Lemon Ricotta Filling

These crepes are best served warm, but they may be chilled until you are ready to use them. If you are chilling them, separate the crepes with plastic wrap or parchment paper to prevent them from sticking together.

1 cup (250 mL) all-purpose flour
2 large eggs
1/2 cup (125 mL) milk
1/2 cup (125 mL) water
1/4 tsp. (1 mL) salt
2 tbsp. (30 mL) butter, melted
2 cups (500 mL) ricotta cheese
1/4 to 1/2 cup (60 to 125 mL) icing (or confectioner's) sugar
2 eggs, beaten
1 lemon, juice and zest

In a large mixing bowl, whisk together flour and eggs. Gradually stir in milk and water. Add salt and butter and beat until smooth. Heat a lightly oiled frying or crepe pan over medium-high heat. Pour 1/4 cup (60 mL) of batter in hot pan. Tilt pan with a circular motion so batter coats surface evenly. Cook crepe for about 2 minutes, until the bottom is light brown. Loosen with a spatula, flip and cook other side. Repeat with remaining batter.

For the filling beat ricotta, icing sugar, eggs and lemon juice in a large bowl, adjusting amount of sugar according to taste. Chill until ready to use. Makes 4 servings.

Wild Grape

Vitus riparia

Also called: riverbank grape

Wild grape is not common in the Prairies and can be found more frequently in more easterly provinces from New Brunswick to Manitoba. Wild grape typically grows in moist thickets and along waterways. This deciduous plant consists of woody vines that trail or climb by clinging tendrils borne along the stem. The leaves resemble the leaves of a maple tree but are more rounded and are toothed at the ends. Wild grape flowers in early June, with inconspicuous light green clusters. When ripe, the small round fruits are dark purple and form a cluster shape similar to cultivated grapes.

Food

Although smaller than cultivated grapes, wild grapes have a unique sourish sweetness and are full of flavour. They can be eaten fresh and are excellent for making juice, wine or jelly. To make juice, place clean, stemmed wild grapes in a large stockpot and pour water over top, but do not fully cover the grapes with water. Bring to a boil on high for about 10 minutes, then turn the heat off and let the mixture stand overnight. The next day, strain the pulp and seeds though a cheesecloth bag. I make jelly from the juice or pour the juice into washed milk jugs and freeze it for later use. This juice can also be used as a base for wine.

The vines can also be used for a fresh, safe, sweet water source. In the growing season, simply cut the vine close to the ground and collect the sap in a container. I have seen birds in the neighbourhood quickly take advantage of this source of water when our vines are pruned in the spring.

Medicine

Traditionally people drank the sap to treat stomach ailments.

Grape Spread

This spread is great on toast with cream cheese or used in place of ketchup.

1 cup (250 mL) water
8 cups (2 L) wild grapes, washed and
    stemmed
2 tbsp. (30 mL) grated orange peel
2 cups (500 mL) granulated sugar
1/2 tsp. (2 mL) ground cinnamon
1/2 tsp. (2 mL) ground cloves
1/4 tsp. (1 mL) ground nutmeg
1/4 tsp. (1 mL) ground ginger

Bring water and grapes to a boil in a large pot, then reduce heat and simmer for 10 minutes. Remove from heat and let stand, covered, on counter overnight to help build flavour. Strain though a colander placed over a bowl and press pulp to further extract juice. Discard pulp. Stir orange peel, sugar and spices into juice. Return to pot and cook mixture over medium heat, stirring constantly, for 10 to 15 minutes or until thick. Pour into sterile jars and seal. Store in refrigerator for up to 1 month. Makes 6 cups (1.5 L).

Grape Jelly

To add a twist to your jelly, add 1 tsp. (5 mL) allspice while it is boiling and let the flavours blend.

5 cups (1.25 mL) of grape juice
3 1/2 cups (875 mL) granulated sugar
1 (2 oz., 57 g) package of pectin

Combine grape juice, sugar and pectin in a large pot and bring to a boil. Reduce heat and simmer until mixture thickens. Pour into sterilized jars. Makes 6 cups (1.5 L).

Meatballs with Chili Grape Sauce

The recipe for the sauce was provided by Ron Heinrichs and Shirley Hauta.

1 lb. (454 g) lean ground beef
9 oz. (250 g) ground pork
1 egg beaten
1/3 cup (75 mL) bread crumbs or
    crushed croutons
3 tbsp. (45 mL) chopped parsley
1/2 cup (125 mL) finely chopped onion
1 garlic clove, minced
1 tsp. (5 mL) Worcestershire sauce
Pepper, to taste
1 tsp. (5 mL) cooking oil
1 1/4 cups (300 mL) grape jelly
1 1/2 cups (375 mL) chili sauce
1 tbsp. (15 mL) lemon juice
2 tbsp. (30 mL) brown sugar, packed
1 tbsp. (15 mL) soy sauce

Combine first 9 ingredients in a large bowl and roll into 1 inch (2.5 cm) balls. Heat oil in a frying pan over medium and brown meatballs.

For the sauce, combine remaining 5 ingredients in a saucepan over medium. Bring to a boil. Reduce heat, add meatballs and simmer for 30 minutes. Makes 5 servings.

Wild grape flower buds

Kinnikinnick

Arctostaphylos uva-ursi

Also called: bearberry, sandberry

A low-growing evergreen shrub, growing up to 10 cm (4") in height, kinnikinnick is found in numerous habitats throughout Canada, often on eroding, dry areas that receive plenty of sunlight. It is a pioneer plant that often grows in dense mats and helps stabilize the soil. It has alternating, leathery, oval leaves and bell-shaped pink flowers that fade to white. Its berries are red, mealy and rather flavourless, though they are high in vitamins A and C. Considered a survival food, these berries preserve well and are easy to find, even under moderate snow cover.

Kinnikinnick in flower

Food
Because of their lack of flavour, kinnikinnick berries are best when cooked in soups, stews and sauces. Kinnikinnick leaves can also be made into tea, but the tea should only be used in moderation as it contains significant amounts of tannin and arbutin, which can cause stomach problems.

Medicine
Tea made from the leaves was traditionally used to treat urinary tract infections and kidney and bladder problems. Cooled tea has been used as a wash for infections.

Other Uses
Some Indigenous peoples have used the leaves in tobacco mixtures, and a natural yellow dye can be extracted from them as well.

Kinnikinnick fruit

Bearberry (Mock Cranberry) Sauce

Try adding cinnamon and cloves for a mock applesauce.

1 cup (250 mL) berries
1/2 cup (125 mL) water
1/2 cup (125 mL) honey

Combine berries and water in a large pot and bring to a boil. Cook for about 10 minutes. Set aside to cool and run berries through a food processor. Return to same pot and add honey. Simmer for 5 minutes. Store in refrigerator for up to 1 week. Makes 1 1/2 cups (375 mL).

Bearberry-ade

2 cups (500 mL) bearberries
2 cups (500 mL) water
3/4 cup (175 mL) honey

Simmer berries, water and honey in a medium pot for 30 minutes. Remove from heat and let stand for 1 hour. Strain mixture, chill and enjoy. Makes 2 1/2 cups (625 mL).

Bearberry Dumplings

1 cup (250 mL) flour
1 tsp. (5 mL) baking powder
Salt, to taste
2 tbsp. (30 mL) lard
1/3 cup (75 mL) milk
2 cups (500 mL) bearberries
1 cup (250 mL) water
2 tbsp. (30 mL) granulated sugar

Mix flour, baking soda and salt in a bowl. Add lard and mix in with your fingers. Stir in milk, and fold in berries. Form dough into small balls. Bring water to a boil in a large pot and stir in sugar. Add dumplings and cook for 20 minutes. Serve hot. Makes 30 dumplings.

Elderberry

Sambucus spp.

Elderberry flower

A member of the honeysuckle family, elderberry is a toxic/purgative plant. This bushy shrub grows 1 to 6 m (3 to 20') high and is characterized by small, tightly clustered berries, which ripen in early summer. The fruit colour is dependent on the species. The outer layer of the twigs is thin and woody, whereas the inside has a thick core of white pith. The leaves, bark and roots are poisonous. The fruit from a few species in the *Sambucus* genus is edible when raw, including the blue elder *(S. cerulean)*, found in southern British Columbia, and Canada elder *(S. canadensis)*, found mostly in eastern Canada. The red elderberry *(S. racemosa* ssp. *pubens)* is found across Canada and is listed as a rare plant in Saskatchewan but not in Alberta or Manitoba according to a search of provincial databases. The extremely bitter fruit of red elderberry is also poisonous when the fruit is raw. Cultivars of elderberry are common, including European varieties, many of which have escaped cultivation. I have an elderberry cultivar in my yard, likely brought in by birds dropping seed.

Food

Fruit from the red elderberry is edible once it is cooked. Elderberry flowers are also edible once they are cooked. They can be used to flavour cooked fruit and jam and make a delicious paring with gooseberries, which are in season at the same time.

Other Uses

Hollowed out stems were used for blowguns and drinking straws; the latter has caused sickness in children.

Elderberry Wine

Feel free to adjust the amount of sugar to suit your taste.

1 lb. (454 g) raisins
6 oz. (170 g) dried elderberries
19 cups (4.75 L) water
3 lbs. (1.4 kg) granulated sugar
2 lemons or oranges
1 1/2 tsp. (7 mL) pectic enzyme
1 tsp. (5 mL) yeast nutrient
1 (0.176 oz., 5 g) package wine yeast
1 campden tablet
1 antioxidant (ascorbic acid) tablet

Elderberry fruit

Chop raisins and combine with next 6 ingredients in a primary fermentation container. Stir until sugar is dissolved. When mixture reaches at least room temperature (ideally 70 to 75°F, 21 to 24°C), sprinkle yeast over surface. Cover with a plastic sheet or lid. Stir daily to re-suspend the surface fruit cap. Ferment for 6 to 7 days in the primary. On day 7, strain out any suspended solids, siphon into a carboy and attach fermentation locks. Rack in 3 weeks and again in about 3 months. When wine is clear and stable (no bubbles) add campden tablet and antioxidant tablet and siphon into sterilized bottles. Wine is best if aged at least 10 months. Makes 1 gal (4.5 L).

sugar water, and then cut lemons into thick slices and add to sugar water. Stir in citric acid. Cover with a clean cloth and leave to steep for 48 hours. Strain into a clean bowl. Pour into sterilized bottles and seal. Store in a cool, dark place (not the refrigerator) for up to 6 weeks. Makes 5 cups (1.25 L).

Elderflower Cordial

5 cups (1.25 L) granulated sugar
6 cups (1.5 L) boiling water
30 large elderflower heads, washed
4 medium lemons
2 oz. (55 g) citric acid

Combine sugar and water in a stockpot and stir until sugar is dissolved. Heat mixture to a slow boil and add flower heads. Cook for 20 minutes, stirring ocaasionally. Remove from heat and set aside to cool. Grate zest of lemons into

Elderflower Vinaigrette

This dressing also makes a good light sauce for fish or baked chicken, or a dressing for hot potatoes.

1/2 cup (125 mL) elderflower cordial
1/2 cup (125 mL) extra virgin olive oil
2 tbsp. (15 mL) white wine vinegar
2 tsp. (10 mL) Dijon mustard
2 tsp. (10 mL) honey

Place all ingredients into a jar with a tight-fitting lid. Shake vigorously until all ingredients are incorporated and creamy. Store in refrigerator for up to 6 weeks. Makes 1 cup (250 mL).

Elderberry Sauce

Use this sauce on meats such as liver. The sauce's flavour improves with age, so wait at least 1 month before using it.

2 cups (500 mL) balsamic vinegar
2 cups (500 mL) elderberries
1 tsp. (5 mL) salt
1/2 tsp. (2 mL) mace
40 peppercorns
12 whole cloves
1 onion, finely chopped
1/2 tsp. (2 mL) ground ginger

Bring vinegar to a boil and pour over elderberries in an oven-safe pot. Cook in 170°F (75°C) oven for at least 6 hours (overnight is even better). Place pot on stove and bring to a boil. Add remaining 6 ingredients and boil for about 10 minutes. Set aside to cool. Pour into sterilized bottles and store in the refrigerator for up to 2 months. Makes 2 cups (500 mL).

Elderberry Ketchup

4 cups (1 L) elderberries
2 cups (500 mL) apple cider vinegar
1/2 cup (125 mL) maple sugar
1/2 tsp. (2 mL) crushed juniper berries
1/2 tsp. (2 mL) ground cinnamon
1 1/2 tsp. (7 mL) ground allspice
1 1/2 tsp. (7 mL) ground cloves
Dried crushed chilies, to taste

Heat berries and vinegar in a heavy saucepan over medium. Bring to a boil, then reduce heat and simmer for 15 minutes. Strain berries through a sieve and return puree to saucepan. Add sugar, juniper, cinnamon, allspice, cloves and chilies. Bring to a rolling boil, then reduce heat to medium and simmer, stirring frequently, for 30 minutes or until thickened. Pour into sterilized jars. Store in refrigerator for up to 3 weeks. Makes 6 1/2 cups (1.6 L).

Elderberry Pie

3 tbsp. (45 mL) cornstarch
1 cup (250 mL) water or fruit punch
4 cups (1 L) elderberries
1 cup (250 mL) granulated sugar
1 tbsp. (15 mL) lemon juice
1 (9 inch, 22 cm) pie shell

Combine cornstarch and water in a small pot over medium heat and stir until thickened. Add berries, sugar and lemon juice. Cook, stirring constantly, until mixture reaches desired thickness. Bake pie shell in 375°F (190°C) oven for about 5 to 7 minutes, so it will not get soggy. Pour berry mixture into shell and bake until browned and the berries are bubbling, about 30 minutes. Cuts into 8 wedges.

High bush cranberry in flower

High Bush Cranberry

Viburnum opulus

This deciduous shrub grows in moist woods, often in riparian areas. It grows up to 4 m (13') in height. The leaves are 3 lobed with a toothed edge. The flowers appear in clusters and are usually white, though they sometimes have a slight pinkish hue. The fruit is a cluster of bright red berries and is quite sour.

Food

The fruit is edible but is sour and astringent. British Columbia has the best tasting varieties, and the fruit is a prized crop in the province. Birds and rodents feed on the fruit. Cranberries are high in vitamin C and are used in baked goods, sauces and jellies. They also complement molasses and toast.

Medicine

Tea made from the bark has been used to treat insomnia.

Cranberry Chocolate Boar Shanks

The boar shanks must marinate overnight, so plan accordingly. Susan Kikcio provided this recipe.

3 cups (750 mL) red wine
4 boar shanks
1 large onion, chopped
1 large carrot
2 stalks celery
6 large juniper berries, crushed
2 large sprigs rosemary
2 sprigs thyme
1 fresh bay leaf (or 2 dried)
1/4 tsp. (1 mL) black peppercorns
1 garlic clove
3 tbsp. (45 mL) olive oil
1/4 cup (60 mL) red wine vinegar
Salt, to taste
Pepper, to taste
2 tbsp. (30 mL) lard
2 oz. (57 g) diced pancetta

1/3 cup (75 mL) granulated sugar
3 tbsp. (45 mL) red wine vinegar
1 cup (250 mL) cranberries
1 oz. (28 g) dark chocolate (70%), chopped

Bring wine to a boil in a large saucepan on high. Reduce heat and simmer until alcohol flavour is cooked out, or carefully light wine with a match to burn off alcohol.

Place shanks in a large deep bowl. Add next 9 ingredients.

Stir olive oil and first amount of red wine vinegar into cooked wine mixture and add to bowl, making sure shanks are thoroughly coated. Cover and refrigerate overnight, turning shanks several times to ensure flavours are infused.

Remove shanks from marinade, pat dry and season with salt and pepper. Strain marinade and set it and strained vegetables, herbs and spices aside. Heat lard in a large roasting pan over a medium-high and brown shanks. Transfer shanks to a plate and set aside.

Cook pancetta in a frying pan over medium heat for about 5 minutes, until fat is rendered. Add vegetables, herbs and spices from marinade and cook for about 10 minutes, until onions begin to colour. Add marinade, bring to a boil and deglaze pan. Return shanks to roasting pan with any juices and add marinade, then cover with a lid. Transfer to 300°F (150°C) oven and cook for 2 1/2 hours, turning shanks once or twice, until meat is almost falling off bone (pork skin can be used to cover shanks at this stage and discarded later when shanks are removed from oven).

While shanks are cooking, heat sugar and remaining red wine vinegar over low heat. When sugar is dissolved, add cranberries and cook, stirring until the they turn to a jam-like consistency. Remove from heat and press though a fine-mesh strainer until you get 1/4 cup (60 mL) liquid. Set liquid aside and discard skins.

Transfer shanks to a plate, cover with foil and set aside to rest. Strain marinade and discard vegetables, herbs and spices. Let liquid stand for 5 minutes and skim off excess fat. Return liquid to frying pan, bring to a boil over high and cook until reduced to about 1 1/2 cups (375 mL). Remove from heat and whisk in chocolate and cranberry mixture. Pour mixture over shanks and serve. Makes 4 servings.

High bush cranberry in fruit

High Bush Cranberry Sauce

For a little variety, try adding some walnuts to taste.

1 cup (250 mL) orange juice or fruit punch
1 1/2 cups (375 mL) granulated sugar
1 tsp. (5 mL) ground cinnamon
1/2 tsp. (2 mL) ground allspice
Ground cloves, to taste
Ground cardamom, to taste
2 tbsp. (30 mL) butter
4 cups (1 L) cranberry

Combine orange juice, sugar, spices and butter in a saucepan over medium. Once sugar is dissolved, add berries and bring to a boil, covered (the berries will start to pop when cooking). Cook for about 5 minutes, until sauce has thickened. Store in refrigerator for up to 2 weeks. Makes 3 1/2 cups (875 mL.)

High Bush Cranberry Pie

Make sure the pie filling is cool before you pour it into the shell or your pie will have a soggy crust.

1/4 cup (60 mL) minute tapioca
Juice of 1 orange
2 cups (500 mL) granulated sugar
3 cups (750 mL) high bush cranberries
1/2 cup (125 mL) raisins
1 tsp. (5 mL) ground cinnamon
1/2 tsp. (2 mL) ground allspice
Ground cloves, to taste
Ground cardamom, to taste
1/4 tsp. (1 mL) orange zest
1 (9 inch, 22 cm) baked pie shell

Combine tapioca and orange juice in a saucepan over medium. Bring to a boil and cook until tapioca is soft. Stir in sugar, berries, raisins, spices and orange zest and bring to a boil. Cook for about 3 minutes. Remove from heat and set aside to cool. Pour cooled mixture into pie shell. Cuts into 8 wedges.

Manitoba Maple

Acer negundo

This species prefers moist soils in ravines and riparian areas including at the edges of streams and riverbanks. It has also been widely used as a shelter-belt tree in the prairies. This deciduous tree can grow to about 12 m (40') in height with stretched-out branches. The bark on young trees is smooth and greyish green. As the tree matures, it becomes grooved and rough as it changes to a dark brown. Leaves are sharp pointed and toothed with shallow lobes.

Food

The sap is boiled down to make syrup. It takes about 40 L (8.8 gal) of sap to make 1 L (4 cups)of syrup. Some sugar evaporates with the water and it may coat everything in your house, so boil the sap outside! The process can be very time consuming but is well worth the effort. Manitoba maple syrup can also be sourced at local farmers' markets.

Medicine

Young twigs were boiled to extract an ingredient for liniments and for snake-bites. Tea from young twigs was used to treat vomiting.

Other Uses

The hardwood is good for making furniture and is excellent as firewood for cooking. Indigenous peoples frequently used young Manitoba maple branches to make snowshoes and bows.

Maple syrup from sugar maple trees (*A. saccharum*) from northeastern North America can also be used for the following recipes.

Maple Butter

This butter is ideal for frying fruit, such as pears, apples and bananas. Cook at a low temperature, as it will burn easily.

1/4 cup (60 mL) butter, softened
2 tbsp. (30 mL) maple syrup

Let butter stand out until it is at room temperature and easy to whip. Whip with a hand blender and slowly add maple syrup. Whip until well mixed. Store in refrigerator for up to 2 weeks. Makes 1/4 cup (60 mL).

Maple Brine Cornish Hen

2 cups (500 mL) chicken stock
1/2 cup (125 mL) maple syrup
1/3 cup (75 mL) brown sugar, packed
3 tbsp. (45 mL) kosher or pickling salt
1 tbsp. (15 mL) dried basil leaves
2 tsp. (10 mL) chopped ginger root
1 tsp. (5 mL) dried crushed chilies
1 tsp. (5 mL) whole peppercorns
1/4 tsp. (1 mL) liquid smoke
1/2 onion, sliced
3 garlic cloves, quartered
2 Cornish hens
1 to 2 tsp. (5 to 10 mL) cornstarch, optional

For the brine, combine first 11 ingredients in a saucepot over medium. Bring to a boil, stirring to dissolve sugar and salt. Simmer for 30 minutes, then remove from heat and set aside too cool. Add Cornish hens and let stand overnight. Remove hens from brine and place on a rack over a pan. Cook in 375°F (190°C) oven for 15 minutes. Reduce heat to 300°F (150°C) and cook for 30 to 40 minutes.

Bring brine to a boil and cook until it thickens, adding cornstarch, if necessary, to help it thicken. Cut hens in half, pour sauce over top and serve. Makes 4 servings.

Maple-Glazed Pork Roast

3 to 4 lb. (1.4 to 1.8 kg) crown pork roast
3 garlic cloves, thinly sliced
1 tsp. (5 mL) finely chopped fresh thyme
Coarse salt, to taste
Pepper, to taste
1/2 cup (125 mL) maple syrup
1/4 cup (60 mL) grainy mustard
1/4 cup (60 mL) cider vinegar

Cut small slits in pork and insert garlic and thyme. Season with salt and pepper. Place roast on a rack in a shallow roasting pan. Cook, uncovered, in 325°F (160°C) oven for 45 minutes. Meanwhile, combine remaining 3 ingredients in a small saucepan and bring to a low boil. Cook until mixture is thickened and reduced by half, about 10 minutes. Brush over pork and cook for about 90 minutes, brushing with glaze every 15 minutes. Let stand for 5 to 7 minutes and drizzle with pan juices before carving. Makes 6 to 8 servings.

Pike with Maple Glaze

This fish tastes best when cooked fresh over a fire.

1/4 cup (60 mL) maple syrup
2 tbsp. (30 mL) hazelnut oil
Kosher salt, to taste
Pepper, to taste
2 juniper berries, crushed
2 lbs. (900 g) northern pike or walleye, filleted and skinned

Combine first 5 ingredients in a small bowl. Grill fish fillets, basting frequently with syrup mixture, for 3 to 4 minutes. Flip fillets and cook second side, basting frequently with syrup, for another 3 to 4 minutes. Makes 2 servings.

Silverberry

Elaeagnus commutata

This plant reaches approximately
1 to 4 m (3 to 13') in height and is widespread, growing on open slopes, flood-
plains and riverbanks, often growing
as an outer mantle beside treed bluffs.
The leaves are silvery green and oval
shaped. The flower is yellow and funnel
shaped, while the berry is silver to light
brown. Edible and sweet, the berry is
also dry and mealy, with a large
brown-and-tan-striped seed.

Silverberry in flower

Food

The berries of this plant have a number of edible uses, even though the
fruit is mealy and dry. Some Indigenous peoples of Alaska fried the fruit
in moose fat, and the Blackfoot Nation
cooked them in soups and used peeled
silverberries to make candy as well as
eating the berries raw.

Medicine

The fruit has traditionally been used
for headache relief.

Other Uses

Along with porcupine quills, Indigenous peoples used the naturally striped
silverberry seeds as beads for jewellery
and decorating. The berries were
boiled to remove the flesh and while
the seeds were still soft, a hole was
pierced from end to end with a hawthorn needle. Silverberry bark was also
used for rope making.

Indigenous peoples consider the
wood unsuitable for burning, as it
has a urine-like odour if burnt while
still green.

Buffaloberry

Shepherdia canadensis

Also called: soapberry

This shrub prefers open woods and riparian areas and grows to about 3 to 5 m (10 to 16') in height. The oval-shaped leaves are opposite to each other and are silvery green. The flowers are yellow and grow in small clusters that ripen into a reddish-orange fruit, much loved by birds. This shrub is found throughout much of the prairies and into the boreal forest. The thorny buffaloberry *(S. argentea)* is similar in appearance but has large thorns and has a more southern prairie distribution.

Buffaloberry in flower

Food

The berries taste best after the first touch of frost and can be used to flavour jellies, refreshments such as buffaloberry-ade and ice cream. You can easily make a natural "slushy" by mixing the berries with sugar, water and a little crushed ice or snow, then shaking the mixture well before serving. I like to mix buffaloberries with sour cherries to make jelly.

Medicine

The berries were traditionally used to treat flu symptoms and as a cool tea for an eye wash.

Thorny buffaloberry in fruit

Simple Buffaloberry Chutney

Serve this chutney with your favourite meats.

1/2 cup (125 mL) buffaloberries
2 tsp. (10 mL) honey

Crush berries until they have the look of ground beef. Add honey and stir until well combined. Store in refrigerator for up to 1 month. Makes 1/2 cup (125 mL).

Buffaloberry-ade

3 cups (750 mL) boiling water
1 cup (250 mL) granulated sugar
1 cup (250 mL) buffaloberries

Blend water with sugar in a medium pot. Heat, stirring, over medium until sugar is dissolved. Stir in berries, and chill in refrigerator for up to 3 days. Pour through a strainer before serving. Makes 4 cups (1 L).

Buffaloberry Ice Cream

1/4 cup (60 mL) apple juice
1 cup (250 mL) buffaloberries
1/4 cup (60 mL) granulated sugar or maple sugar

In a glass bowl whisk apple juice and berries until they start to foam. Gradually add sugar and beat until mixture stiffens. It is important the berries do not come in contacted with grease or they will not foam. Serve immediately. Makes 4 servings.

Buffaloberry Cream Cheese Spread

2 cups (500 mL) buffaloberries
2 tbsp. (30 mL) granulated sugar
1/4 cup (60 mL) water
8 oz. (225 g) cream cheese

Combine berries and sugar in a medium pot. Add just enough water to cover. Cook on medium until softened. Crush berries with a potato masher. Let mixture cool. Blend with cream cheese until smooth. Store in refrigerator for up to 3 weeks. Makes 4 servings.

Chokecherry

Prunus virginiana

This plant grows in a wide variety of soil conditions but prefers moist areas. On the prairie, it is often found in bunches or on the edges of bluffs. The plant varies from a shrub to a small tree in size. The bark is reddish brown. Leaves are a long oval shape with pointed tips. The flowers are white and form a cone-shaped cluster.

Food

The fruit is often used to make jelly, syrup and wine. In Europe, the fruit is used to make a soup that can be served warm with a dab of sour cream or converted into a dessert by serving it cold with whipped cream.

Chokecherry was an important fruit to Indigenous peoples of the plains, perhaps second only to the saskatoon berry. Both berries were used in pemmican and were also blended into animal fat and put on flatbreads. For pemmican, the bison meat was sliced thin and smoked. The meat was pounded into a powder with a few fibrous pieces remaining to hold the mixture together when the cherries and berries were pounded into the meat. The pits of the cherry were left in and were crushed into the meat, which helped blend in the fruit. The pemmican was placed on sun-drying racks. The seed in the cherry pits is poisonous; however, exposing the seed to sunlight in the drying process dissipated the poison.

Medicine

Bark from the chokecherry and other *Prunus* species was used as a traditional and folk medicine to treat coughs and stomach ailments, but this is not advised (see Warning, below).

WARNING: The leaves, pits and bark of *Prunus* species are poisonous. Consuming large quantities of cherry pits or chewing cherry twigs has led to poisoning and fatalities.

Other Uses

The chokecherry plant had many other uses, as well. The dense wood burns well and provides lasting heat. Straight, thin branches were used to make shafts for arrows and also made good roasting sticks. Thicker branches were used as digging sticks for root crops. The fruit was also used for paint in rock pictographs.

On one occasion, I accidentally blended frozen chokecherries along with frozen wild grapes, thinking they were all chokecherries. I'm not sure of the cherry to grape ratio I used, but the resulting jelly was excellent.

Chokecherry Soup

4 cups (1 L) water
4 cups (1 L) chokecherries
Granulated sugar, to taste
Salt, to taste

In a medium pot, bring water to a simmer. Add chokecherries and simmer for 30 minutes. Lightly crush chokecherries with a potato masher and run mashed fruit through a strainer into another pot. Do not crush pits. Simmer chokecherries again for a few minutes. Add sugar and salt to taste. For a soup, serve hot with a spoonful of sour cream. For a dessert, serve cold and top with whipped cream. Makes 6 servings.

Chokecherry Jelly

4 cups (1 L) of chokecherries
1/2 cup (125 mL) water
2 tbsp. (30 mL) lemon juice
1 (2 oz., 57 g) package of pectin
1 1/2 cups (375 mL) granulated sugar

Combine chokecherries and water in a large pot and bring to a boil. Reduce heat and simmer, covered, until soft, about 1 hour. Drain and mash chokecherries with a potato masher, taking care not to crush pits. Use a jelly bag or fine-mesh strainer to strain mixture into another pot. Add remaining 3 ingredients and bring to a slow boil until mixture thickens. Pour jelly into sterilized jars and let set. Makes 6 cups (1.5 L).

Raspberry

Rubus idaeus

This perennial, circumpolar shrub, which usually reaches about 90 cm to 1.2 m (3 to 4') in height, grows in thickets, open woods and riparian areas. It usually flowers in July, producing white blossoms with 5 petals on stems bristled with thorns. Raspberry fruit is bright red when ripe.

Food
Dried leaves and berries are useful for teas. The fruit is good eaten raw and cooked in jams, pies and other baked goods.

Medicine
Traditionally the leaves were used to treat abdominal cramps.

Chilled Raspberry Soup

2 cups (500 mL) raspberries
Vanilla extract, to taste
1 1/2 cups (375 mL) granulated sugar
1 cup (250 mL) cream
1/2 cup (125 mL) milk

Blend all 5 ingredients in a blender until smooth. Serve chilled. Makes 4 servings.

Raspberry Vinegar

4 cup (1 L) raspberries
1 cup (250 mL) apple cider vinegar
3/4 cup (175 mL) granulated sugar

Combine raspberries and vinegar in a large bowl. Cover and let stand in refrigerator for 4 days. Transfer to a medium pot and bring to a boil. Add sugar and cook for about 10 minutes, until sugar is dissolved. Strain mixture, discarding pulp. Bottle vinegar in sterilized jars. Store in a cool, dark place for up to 3 months. Makes 5 cups (1.25 L).

Raspberry flower

Saskatoon in flower

Saskatoon Berry

Amelanchier alnifolia

Also called: juneberry, serviceberry

This plant is often found in thickets, open woods and along streams and riverbanks. It grows between a shrub and a small tree in size and produces a white flower cluster as early as April. The bark is dark grey, and the toothed leaves are oval, or nearly round. The saskatoon plant is a member of the rose family and is related to the apple, which the berries of the saskatoon closely resemble. Fruit production varies greatly and is dependent on weather conditions, especially at the flowering stage. The berries are high in iron and copper, similar to raisins and prunes, and have become a highly prized commercial crop.

Saskatoon berry resembling apple in cross-section.

There are at least 15 different species of saskatoon berry in Canada, with the most abundant and perhaps well-known species being the western *A. alnifolia*. Other saskatoon berry species are found in eastern Canada. The name "saskatoon" is derived from the Cree word *mis-sask-quah-toomina* and is how the city of Saskatoon got its name. The plant is abundant in the Saskatoon area, especially along riverbanks, and was a staple for Indigenous peoples and early settlers. During the original town survey, the local Indigenous peoples gathered the berries and sold them, calling out what sounded like "saskatoons" to the surveyors (Turner and Szczawinski, 1988: 137).

Food

The berries were dried for winter storage and were often cooked with bear grease and various root crops for soups, stews and pemmican. Today, saskatoon berries are popular in pies, jams, syrups and wine.

Medicine

Stems and roots were boiled into tea and used to treat lung issues such as tuberculosis and lung infections as well as coughs, colds and fevers.

Other Uses

The young, straight shoots of the saskatoon were used to make arrow shafts.

Saskatoon Chutney

Serve this chutney with your favourite meats.

2 tbsp. (30 mL) vegetable oil
1 large onion, chopped
1 finely chopped jalapeño, seeds removed
2 tsp. (10 mL) minced garlic
1 medium red pepper
2 tsp. (10 mL) minced ginger root
1 tsp. (5 mL) turmeric
1/2 tsp. (2 mL) ground cinnamon
1/2 tsp. (2 mL) ground allspice
1/4 tsp. (1 mL) dried crushed chilies
3 cups (750 mL) saskatoon berries
1/4 cup (60 mL) brown sugar, packed
1/4 cup (60 mL) balsamic or apple cider vinegar
1/4 cup (60 mL) mint

Heat oil in a saucepan over medium. Add onion and jalapeño and cook until tender. Add garlic, red pepper, ginger root and spices and cook until fragrant. Add berries, sugar, vinegar and mint and simmer until mixture thickens. Set aside to cool. Store in a sealed glass jar in refrigerator for up to 2 weeks.

Saskatoon fruit

Hawthorn berries

Wild Hawthorn

Crataegus spp.

This plant grows in moist to dry soils in thickets. It is a tall shrub that may grow to 4 m (13'). The stem has thorns 3 to 7 cm (1 1/4 to 2 3/4") in length. The 5-petal, white flowers form in clusters from May to June. The fruit is red and resembles a rose hip but is often larger and full of seeds. The toothed leaves are alternating, dark green and oval to palmately lobed in shape.

Food
Hawthorn berries are delicious in sauces and jellies. Hawthorn candies are commercially available.

Medicine
The berry has properties useful in heart medications but should be used cautiously.

Other Uses
Traditional tools made of hawthorn spines included needles for sewing and awls for punching holes in skins. Indigenous peoples also used hawthorn spines as fishhooks to catch an extensive variety of fish, including large sturgeons. Be cautious around hawthorn bushes as thorn scratches to the eyes may cause blindness.

Hawthorn Sauce

This sauce is great on ham or chicken.

4 cups (1 L) fruit punch juice
1 cup (250 mL) plums
2 1/2 cups (625 mL) hawthorn fruit
1 1/2 tbsp. (22 mL) whole allspice
1 1/2 tbsp. (22 mL) ground cloves
Salt, to taste
1/2 tsp. (2 mL) cayenne
2 1/2 cups (625 mL) granulated sugar
4 cups (1 L) apple cider vinegar

Boil fruit punch, plums and hawthorn
fruit until fruit is soft. Rub fruit through
a sieve to remove seeds and return to
pot. Tie allspice and cloves in a cheese-
cloth and add to fruit mixture. Stir in
remaining 4 ingredients. Bring to a boil
and cook until thickened. Remove spice
bag and pour mixture into sterilized jars.
Makes 6 cups (1.5 L)

Hawthorn thorn

Ripening plum

Wild Plum

Prunus spp.

This small tree of the rose family prefers river valleys and limestone-enriched soils. The only wild plums I have seen growing in the wild were at Saskatchewan Landing, but the plum is apparently becoming more common across Canada through its use as an ornamental and/or fruit tree or by escaping cultivation. Plum trees are very scraggly looking and grow crooked, the branches spreading out from a more or less central crown. They can grow up

Plum tree blossoms

to about 8 m (26') high. Although several plum species have been introduced, only 2 wild plum species are known to grow in the prairies, including the Canada plum *(P. nigra)*, in southern Manitoba and eastward, and the American plum *(P. americana)*, which is found in Saskatchewan, Manitoba and Ontario. Both species appear similar; however, the bark of the Canada plum is black, whereas the bark of the American plum is dark reddish brown to grey, with both species having short horizontal markings. Both species have oval shaped leaves; the Canada plum leaves are generally wider and are often broadest towards the tip, whereas the American plum leaves are widest below the middle. The plentiful fragrant flowers, which appear just as the leaves are budding out in spring, are more whitish in the American plum and are a whitish to pink hue in the Canada plum. The blossoms form loose clusters of about 3 to 5 flowers and are very showy. The early fruit has an orange-purple hue and is about 2.5 cm (1") in length with a whitish waxy coating on the American plum. The plum becomes ripe in late summer to early fall. The fruit is juicy and sweet when ripe. The American plum is listed as a rare plant in Saskatchewan and Manitoba, accord-ing to a recent search of provincial databases. This plant may be listed elsewhere. As noted previously, you should check the status of your target plants to determine whether or not they are rare; this may vary from province to province, and from year to year.

Food

The fruit can be eaten raw or cooked is used in jams, jellies, sauces and baked goods.

WARNING: The large, flat pit is poisonous.

Chicken Thighs in Plum Sauce

2 tbsp. (30 mL) cooking oil
1 onion, coarsely chopped
4 garlic cloves, coarsely chopped
1 tbsp. (15 mL) ginger root, coarsely chopped
1 chili pepper, coarsely chopped
1/4 tsp. (1 mL) ground cinnamon
1/4 tsp. (1 mL) ground cloves
1 1/2 lbs. (680 g) red or purple plums, pitted and coarsely chopped
1/4 cup (60 mL) honey
1/4 cup (60 mL) soy sauce
2 tbsp. (30 mL) fresh lime juice
1 tbsp. (15 mL) granulated sugar
8 bone-in chicken thighs, skin on
Salt, to taste
Pepper, to taste

Heat oil in a saucepan over medium-high. Add onion and garlic and cook until soft. Add ginger root, chili pepper, cinnamon and cloves and cook for 2 minutes. Add next 5 ingredients and cook until plums are soft and mixture has thickened. Place mixture in a food processor and process until smooth. Set aside to cool.

Preheat grill. Season chicken with salt and pepper. Grill chicken on first side for 5 minutes, or until golden brown. Turn over, brush with plum sauce and con-tinue grilling for 3 to 4 minutes. Turn over again and brush with sauce. Con-tinue grilling, alternately turning and brushing with sauce, until chicken is cooked through, about 12 to 15 min-utes. Makes 5 servings.

Plum Pudding

5 cups (1.25 L) plums
3 tbsp. (45 mL) confectioners' sugar
2 cinnamon sticks
2 stars of anise
2 vanilla beans
1 tbsp. (15 mL) orange zest
1 cup (250 mL) stock syrup (see recipe below)
1 cup (250 mL) light corn syrup
1 cup (250 mL) whipped cream or yogurt

Halve plums and remove pits. Set aside a couple of plums to use as a topping. In a heavy-based pot combine remaining plums, sugar, spices and orange zest and cook over medium for 30 minutes. Add stock syrup and corn syrup and bring to a boil. Reduce heat and simmer for 15 minutes. Remove cinnamon, vanilla beans and star anise. Set aside to cool. Purée cooled mixture in a blender. Serve topped with sliced plums and whipped cream or yogurt. Makes 6 servings.

Stock Syrup

2 1/2 cups (625 mL) rock sugar or raw sugar
2 cups (500 mL) water

In a heavy-based pot, dissolve sugar in water over low heat. Bring to a boil and cook for about 5 minutes. Cool and keep in the refrigerator for up to 2 weeks. Makes 2 1/4 cups (550 mL).

Plum Ketchup

8 1/2 cups (2.1 L) pitted plums
1/4 cup (60 mL) fruit punch
1/2 tsp. (2 mL) baking soda
1 1/3 cups (325 mL) maple syrup
4 cups (1 L) granulated sugar
1 cup (250 mL) apple cider vinegar
1 1/4 tsp. (6 mL) ground cloves
1 1/2 tsp. (7 mL) ground allspice
1/2 tsp. (2 mL) ground nutmeg
1/2 tsp. (2 mL) pepper
3/4 tsp. (4 mL) ground cinnamon

In a large pot, combine plums, fruit juice and baking soda. Bring to a boil and cook for about 30 minutes, until fruit breaks down enough to run though a strainer. Strain mixture in a fine-mesh sieve to remove skins and pits. Return to a medium heat, add remaining ingredients and simmer until thickened. Pour into sterilized jars and let set. Store in refrigerator for up to 3 months. Makes 8 cups (2 L).

Lamb Shanks with Plum

1/4 cup (60 mL) flour
Salt, to taste
Pepper, to taste
1/2 tsp. (2 mL) finely chopped bergamot leaves
4 lamb shanks
2 cups (500 mL) plums, pitted and chopped
1 cup (250 mL) chicken stock
1/4 cup (60 mL) balsamic vinegar
1/2 tsp. (2 mL) ground cinnamon
1/2 tsp. (2 mL) ground allspice
1 tbsp. (15 mL) cornstarch

Combine flour, salt, pepper and bergamot on a shallow plate. Coat lamb shanks with mixture. Bake lamb a large greased baking dish in 350°F (175°C) oven for 2 hours.

(continued on next page)

Lamb Shanks with Plum

Combine next 5 ingredients in a saucepot and simmer for 15 to 20 minutes so flavours blend. Remove baking dish from oven. Transfer lamb to a plate and set aside. Drain and discard grease from baking dish. Pour plum sauce into baking dish and stir, scraping browned bits from bottom of dish. Place lamb back in dish and bake for another 30 minutes.

Remove dish from oven and transfer lamb to a plate. In a bowl, stir cornstarch and 4 or 5 tbsp. (60 to 75 mL) sauce from baking dish until smooth to make a roux. Pour roux into baking dish and stir to thicken. Place lamb back in dish and cook for another 10 minutes. Makes 4 servings.

Chipotle Plum Barbeque Sauce

6 cups (1.5 L) pitted plums
3 medium onions
3 garlic cloves, minced
1 tbsp. (15 mL) chipotle chili powder
1 tbsp. (15 mL) smoked paprika
1/2 cup (125 mL) cider vinegar
Granulated sugar, to taste
Salt, to taste

Combine first 3 ingredients in a food processor, or finely chop and add to a heavy-bottomed saucepan. Stir in next 3 ingredients and simmer until mixture thickens. Remove from heat, season with sugar and salt. Pour into sterilized jars and store in refrigerator for up to 3 months. Makes 5 cups (1.25 mL).

Wild Prickly Rose

Rosa acicularis

This common thorny shrub grows in thickets, depressions, riparian areas, open woods and fields. The leaves are oval and toothed. The flowers are a light to dark pink with 5 petals and are very fragrant. The fruit is a bright red hip and contains several seeds on the inside. Other similar species found on the prairies include the less armoured wood rose *(R. woodsii)* and the diminutive subshrub, prairie rose *(R. arkansana)*.

Wild rose flower

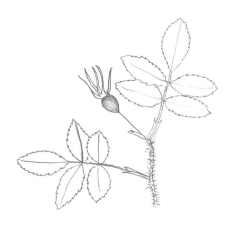

Food

Middle Eastern cultures use the rose petals to make rose water for desserts or refreshments. The petals add a fragrant flavour when steeped in honey and can be made into a syrup or vinegar for cooking. The fruit is high in vitamin C; 3 rosehips have more vitamin C than an orange. The hip also contains vitamin A, calcium, phosphorus and iron. For raw hips, it is best to eat only the outside part of the hip and avoid the seeds in the centre. If you eat too many seeds, which have tiny barbs, you will probably have digestive discomfort and will find out why some Indigenous peoples call the hips "itchy bum berries"—but your colon will likely be really well scrubbed out. From the hips, you can also make syrup, refreshments and jelly, and dried hips can be made into tea.

Medicine

Traditionally the lower stems and roots were made into a tea for colds and coughs. Cool tea was used as an eye wash for snow blindness.

Other Uses

This plant has many diverse uses, including integration into commercial perfumes.

Rosehip Jelly

For additional flavour, try adding 2/3 cup (150 mL) bergamot flower petals and young leaves while the mixture is still boiling.

8 cups (2 L) rosehips
6 cups (1.5 L) fruit punch or apple juice
1/2 cup (125 mL) lemon juice
1 (2 oz., 57 g) package of pectin
1/4 tsp. (1 mL) butter
3 1/2 cups (875 mL) granulated sugar

Combine rosehips and fruit punch in a large pot and bring to a boil. Reduce heat and simmer, covered, for 1 hour until rosehips are soft. Mash with a potato masher. To remove seeds, use a jelly bag or a fine-mesh strainer to strain mixture into another pot. Add remaining 4 ingredients and bring to a slow boil until mixture thickens. Pour into sterilized jars and seal. Makes about 6 cups (1.5 L).

Rosehip Marmalade

This recipe is a variation of the rosehip jelly recipe. The rosehips transform into a candy-like treat in the marmalade.

8 cups (2 L) rosehips
6 cups (1.5 L) fruit punch or apple juice
1/2 cup (125 mL) lemon juice
1 (2 oz., 57 g) package of pectin
1/4 tsp. (1 mL) butter
5 cups (1.25 L) granulated sugar
1 large orange, peeled and cubed
1 cup (250 mL) rose hips, with ends cut off and seeds pushed out
1 medium green apple, peeled and grated

Combine rosehips and fruit punch in a large pot and bring to a boil. Reduce heat and simmer, covered, for 1 hour until rosehips are soft. Mash with a potato masher. To remove seeds, use a jelly bag or a fine-mesh strainer to strain mixture into another pot. Add remaining 7 ingredients and bring to a slow boil until mixture thickens. Pour into sterilized jars and seal. Makes about 6 cups (1.5 L).

Wild rosehip

Roasted Chicken with Rose-hip and Raspberry Sauce

You can use pork instead of chicken in this recipe, if you prefer.

1 whole chicken (about 4 lbs., 1.8 kg)
Salt, to taste
Pepper, to taste
1 cup (250 mL) red wine
1 tbsp. (15 mL) rosehip jelly
1 vanilla bean
1 whole star anise
2 tbsp. (30 mL) finely cut white onion
1/2 cup (125 mL) raspberries

Season chicken with salt and pepper and cook in 350°F (175°C) oven for about 2 hours, until cooked through. Transfer chicken to a large plate and set aside, keeping it warm.

Deglaze roasting pan with wine, scraping browned bits from bottom of pan. Stir in remaining 5 ingredients and cook for 3 to 5 minutes. Remove vanilla bean and star anise. Whisk mixture into a sauce, pour over chicken and serve. Makes 4 servings.

Rose Petal Honey

Use rose petal honey along with rosemary on a roasted chicken, basting for the last 10 minutes of cooking to give the meat a unique flavour.

1 cup (250 mL) fresh wild rose petals
1 cup (250 mL) honey

Place rose petals and honey in a small pot and bring to a boil. Remove from heat and let stand for about 10 minutes to cool. Strain out rose petals and pour honey into a jar. Makes 1 cup (250 mL) honey.

Wild rosehip

Plains Cottonwood Poplar

Populus deltoides

This tree grows in moist rich soil, often along waterways, reaching a height of 20 to 40 m (65 to 130'). The leaves are oval shaped and toothed, coming to a point at the tip. The flowers are catkins, and when mature the seeds readily disperse in the wind, being attached to fluffy cotton-like strands.

Cottonwood leaf; similar to a tipi shape as the leaf curls up.

Other Uses

The cottonwood was important to the survival of Indigenous peoples living on the plains and prairies. It was used for practical purposes such as firewood and may have been beneficial for other critical aspects of survival, including shelter and water. The roots of cottonwoods found on the banks of dried-up streambeds often lead down to water under the ground's surface or indicate where to look for water.

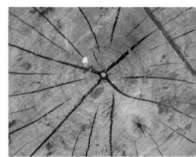

Cottonwood log; the cracking pattern resembles the Morning Star

This tree is considered sacred to many plains and prairie cultures. According to their traditions, cottonwood leaves helped teach principles of shelter building; when the yellow leaves fall in autumn, they curl up on the ground and resemble miniature tipis, equipped with an open end for smoke from a fire to exit. In other plains and prairie traditions, the cottonwood serves as the center pole for the Sun Dance ceremony. Cottonwood is an easy wood to carve, and a star shape symbolizing the sacred Morning Star is visible in the centre of a cut log.

To attract animals, Indigenous hunters often used the buds of the cottonwood, which are sought after for browsing by a variety of plant eating wildlife. Young leaves and buds of the cottonwood tree are sticky with resin, and along with beeswax, were used to waterproof hides.

Sandbar willow

Juvenile sandbar willow

Willow

Salix spp.

This diverse genus generally prefers moist areas. The willow is a deciduous shrub to small tree, usually growing 2 to 6 m (7 to 20') in height, though some species grow considerably taller.

The flowers usually consist of tiny fuzzy clusters, often called catkins or pussy willows, with male and female catkins growing on different shrubs. When young, the bark is often greenish yellow. As it matures, the bark becomes darker. Sandbar willow *(S. interior)* has long, narrow leaves that are toothed at the ends.

Medicinal Use

The bark contains acetylsalicylic acid, an ingredient commonly found in commercially available pain-relief medications. This ingredient has also been used to treat heart conditions.

Other Uses

The plant branch remains very elastic even after being cut and has been used by Indigenous peoples to make fire bows— short bows for starting friction fires.

Grasses, Herbs, Forbs and Weedy Plants of the Prairies

Most of us are familiar with at least a few of the popular treats from herbaceous plants of the Prairies, such as strawberries, wild mint or even wild asparagus. It is likely, though, that fewer people have heard of, much less tried, fireweed soup or a wildflower salad, or have added weeds to the menu. The mix of foods you might find from herbaceous plants on the trail includes leaves, flowers, fruits, seeds, stems and roots. The following chapter highlights a few of these favourites as well as several not-so-familiar plants, along with suggested recipes and culinary ideas.

Canada Goldenrod

Solidago canadensis

Found in open woods and meadows, growing from 30 cm to 2 m (1 to 7') in height, this perennial plant has narrow, lanced-shaped leaves. The flowers are dense and made up of tiny, yellow flower clusters.

Food

All aerial parts of the plant can be used. Eaten raw or cooked in soups or stews, the young plants are good as a green vegetable, similar to spinach. Fresh flowers are edible and make attractive garnishes for salads, whereas dried flowers and leaves make a pleasant tea. The seed is "fluffy" and can be ground into a fine powder and used as a starch or thickening agent in soups and stews.

Medicine

Dried flowers make a soothing tea for stomach-ailments. Goldenrod oil can be used as a topical for muscle cramps.

Strawberry Goldenrod Pesto

The stringy mid-vein of the goldenrod leaves may resist processing; just use a spatula or spoon to stir the contents of the food processor occasionally between pulses.

1 cup (250 mL) Canada goldenrod leaves

1/4 cup (60 mL) sliced almonds

1/3 cup (75 mL) olive oil

1 tbsp. (15 mL) lemon juice

1 1/2 cups (375 mL) fresh strawberries with tops removed

1 tsp. (5 mL) salt

1 tsp. (5 mL) pepper

Combine goldenrod, almonds, olive oil and lemon juice in a food processor and pulse until you have a chunky paste. Add strawberries a few at a time and pulse until creamy. Add salt and pepper and mix briefly. Chill and serve cool. Makes 4 servings.

Goldenrod in flower

Jerusalem artichoke in flower

Jerusalem Artichoke

Helianthus tuberosus

Also called: sun choke

This plant is a tall-growing perennial and is related to the common sunflower. The plant is native to North America and typically grows to about 2 to 3 m (7 to 10') in height. The leaves are oval, toothed and pointed at the end. The leaves and stock have a rough, hairy texture. Several to numerous yellow flowers, resembling small common sunflowers, form at the upper portions of the plant. The roots produce edible tubers, usually golf ball to walnut sized, often in clusters. In eastern North America, the plant has become a common weed in many places, including wastelands, roadsides and abandoned gardens (Szczawinski and Turner, 1988). The plant regenerates each year from the tubers left in the ground. The plant is listed as rare in Saskatchewan and Manitoba, but not in Alberta, according to a recent search of prairie provincial databases.

79

Food

Indigenous peoples cultivated this plant as a food source. Settlers later used it as well, and it became more widespread. The tubers are best harvested in the fall after the first frost and when the tops have shut down for the winter. The tubers stay fresh and firm when stored in a pail of sand indoors throughout the winter.

The tubers taste similar to a potato but are somewhat sweeter because of the presence of inulin, which is a complex sugar. The tubers contain very little starch, so they may be suitable for diabetics who require a low-starch diet (Szczawinski and Turner, 1988).

These tubers can be used in place of potatoes or can be added to mashed potatoes, and they are great raw in salads. The tubers do not need to be peeled but should be scrubbed clean before eating.

Roasted Jerusalem Artichokes with Garlic and Rosemary

6 1/2 cups (1.5 L) Jerusalem artichoke
   tubers
1 garlic bulb
1 tbsp. (15 mL) rosemary
3 tbsp. (45 mL) grapeseed oil
Salt, to taste
Pepper, to taste
Ground mace, to taste
1 tbsp. (15 mL) butter
2 tsp. (10 mL) lemon juice

Soak tubers in cold water for 20 minutes to help loosen dirt, then scrub with a scourer to remove any grit. Place tubers in a shallow roasting pan, cutting larger ones in half. Cut top off garlic bulb and cut bulb in half, and add it to pan along with rosemary. Pour oil over top, season with salt and pepper and stir to coat. Cook in 350°F (175°C) oven for 45 to 50 minutes, until tubers are tender and crispy on outside. Remove garlic from pan and squeeze softened garlic cloves from their skins. Mash cloves and add to roasted artichokes along with mace, butter and lemon juice. Makes 4 servings.

Jerusalem Artichoke Soup

2 tbsp. (30 mL) butter
1 cup (250 mL) chopped onion
1 celery root, chopped
2 large garlic cloves, chopped
Salt, to taste
4 cups (1 L) Jerusalem artichokes,
   peeled and quartered
4 cups (1 L) homemade chicken
   stock or vegetable broth
Pepper, to taste

Heat butter in a stockpot over medium-high and cook onions and celery root until soft and slightly browned. Add garlic and cook for 1 minute. Sprinkle with salt. Add Jerusalem artichokes and chicken stock bring to a simmer. Cook until Jerusalem artichokes begin to break down, about 1 hour. Set aside for a few minutes to cool. Transfer to a blender and puree soup. Reheat if desired and sprinkle with freshly grated pepper to serve. Makes 5 servings.

Prairie Sage

Artemisia ludoviciana

Prairie sage is very aromatic, with narrow, greyish-green alternate leaves covered in soft, woolly hairs. This plant often forms dense colonies and is found growing in fields and prairie grasslands, reaching 50 to 70 cm (20 to 28") in height. Sage flowers are summer-blooming clusters of yellow disk-like blossoms.

Food
Sage is an herb popular for flavouring meats, soups and stews.

Medicine
As well as cooking with sage, plains Indigenous peoples have used sage to cover sweat lodge floors and to "smudge," a sacred ritual of purification using smoke as incense for spiritual cleansing. During the ceremony, sage is braided and burnt to purify and protect the persons and ceremonial area from negative influences. Interestingly, the botanical name for common sage, a subshrub native to the Mediterranean and naturalized elsewhere, is *Salvia officinalis*, which comes from the Latin root word *salvare*, meaning "to heal."

Apple Sage Soup

Apple Sage Soup

2 tbsp. (30 mL) unsalted butter

3 medium onions, finely chopped

3 medium Granny Smith apples, peeled, cored, and cut into 1/4" (6 mm) slices

Salt, to taste

6 cups (1.5 L) chicken stock

1/4 cup (60 mL) apple cider or apple juice

1 bay leaf

Pepper, to taste

1 tbsp. (15 mL) finely chopped fresh sage

6 slices bacon

1 cup (250 mL) grated sharp old Cheddar cheese

1 French baguette, cut on the bias into about twelve 1/2" (12 mm) slices

Heat butter in a large stockpot over low. Add onion, apple and salt and stir until well coated with butter. Cook slowly over low heat, stirring frequently, until onion and apple are deeply caramelized and bottom of pot is coated with a dark brown crust, about 30 minutes. Stir in chicken stock, apple cider and bay leaf. Bring to a boil and scrape bottom of pot with a wooden spoon to loosen brown crust. Simmer for 20 minutes to blend flavors. Discard bay leaf and season with pepper. Stir in chopped sage and simmer.

Cook bacon until crispy. Drain and let cool, then chop and mix with cheese.

Place oven-proof soup crocks on a rimmed baking sheet. Fill each crock almost to top with soup. Top each with 2 baguette slices and sprinkle with cheese-bacon mixture. Place baking sheet in oven and broil until cheese is bubbling and well browned, about 2 to 4 minutes. Makes 5 servings.

Butternut Squash Soup

When pureeing this soup, depending on the style of your blender, you may want to remove the small cap from the blender lid (the pouring lid) and cover the space with a kitchen towel. This will allow steam to escape and prevent the lid from popping off.

4 pounds (1.8 kg) whole butternut squash (about 2 medium), halved lengthwise and seeds removed

3 tbsp. (45 mL) unsalted butter
1 tsp. (5 mL) ground ginger
3/4 cup (175 mL) apple juice
2 Granny Smith apples, peeled, cored
　and chopped (about 2 cups, 500 mL)
1 tbsp. (15 mL) butter
1 medium onion, finely chopped
8 fresh sage leaves
Salt, to taste
Pepper, to taste
2 1/2 cups (625 mL) chicken stock
1/3 cup (75 mL) heavy cream
1/2 cup (125 mL) toasted pumpkin
　seeds, for garnish (optional)

Place squash halves in a baking dish, cut side up. Spread first amount of butter in cavities and sprinkle with ginger. Pour apple juice over top until cavity is full. Cover dish with aluminum foil and roast in 425°F (220°C) oven until tender, about 50 minutes to 1 hour.

Heat remaining butter in a large saucepan. Add apple, onion, sage, salt and pepper. Cook, stirring occasionally, until softened, about 7 minutes. Remove from heat and set aside. Scoop flesh of cooled squash from skins and add to apple mixture. Add chicken stock and any remaining apple juice and bring to a boil over medium-high. Reduce heat to medium-low and simmer, stirring occasionally and breaking up any large pieces of squash, for about 15 minutes. Remove from heat and stir in cream. Puree soup in batches until mixture is smooth. Serve garnished with toasted pumpkin seeds. Makes 5 servings.

Apple Cheddar Sage Soup

1 tbsp. (45 mL) butter
1 tbsp. (15 mL) olive oil
3 Granny Smith apples peeled, cored
　and chopped (about 3 cups, 750 mL)
1 medium onion, diced
2 parsnips, diced
1 medium carrot, diced

3 garlic cloves, minced
1/2 tsp. (2 mL) chopped sage
2 cups (500 mL) apple juice
1/4 tsp. (1 mL) pepper
2 tbsp. (30 mL) butter
2 tbsp. (30 mL) potato flour
1 cup (250 mL) milk, warmed
1 cup (250 mL) grated aged cheddar
　cheese
1 tsp. (5 mL) kosher salt

Heat first amount of butter and olive oil in a heavy saucepan over medium. Add next 5 ingredients and cook, stirring occasionally, until golden brown. Add sage, apple juice and pepper and simmer for about 15 minutes. Set aside to cool. Puree in a blender.

Combine remaining butter, potato flour and milk in a saucepan over medium. Cook, stirring, until sauce thickens. Stir in cheese and apple/vegetable mixture and salt. Serve with sage croutons, below. Makes 5 servings.

Sage Croutons

2 tbsp. (30 mL) butter
1 tbsp. (15 mL) olive oil
3 sage leaves, finely chopped
2 cups (500 mL) 2.5 cm (1") focaccia
　bread cubes
Salt, to taste
Pepper, to taste

Heat butter and oil in a saucepan over medium. When butter has melted, but before it gets too hot, add sage. Place bread cubes in a large bowl. Add sage butter and toss until bread cubes are coated. Season with salt and pepper. Spread onto a baking sheet lined with parchment paper and bake in 350°F (175°C) oven for 15 to 20 minutes. Makes 2 cups (500 mL).

Dock

Rumex occidentalis

Dock in flower

This plant is a rhubarb relative in the buckwheat family. There are many species in the *Rumex* genus, including the common western dock *(R. occidentalis)*. Dock prefers disturbed soils, roadsides and moist areas and grows to 50 cm to 1. 5 m (20" to 5') in height. This robust plant has long, large leaves at the base, which become reduced in the upper portion of the plant. The leaves alternate in a circular growing pattern and have a coarse texture. Dock typically has tiny green flowers growing in dense heads along a spire. As the plant ages, older leaves change colour, often developing a red hue to their primary vein, as do the flowers, which later change to a reddish brown. Seed wings are triangular or heart shaped with several dark brown seed heads. Curled or curly dock *(R. crispus)* is from Europe and is naturalized in Canada. This plant has somewhat more narrow leaves with wavy to curled edges and is a biennial plant, which means it takes 2 years to reach the flowering stage.

Food

As a green vegetable, dock cooks like spinach and is good with muffins or mixed with cheese. Younger leaves are best. Dock is high in vitamins A and C and is a source of iron and potassium. Consume in moderation as it contains oxalic acids, which can cause internal irritation in larger amounts.

Medicine

Rub dock leaves on skin affected by nettle stings to relieve itching and burning.

Dock Muffins

Dock Muffins

For additional flavour, I like to add bacon to the mixture.

2 tbsp. (30 mL) butter
1 cup (250 mL) chopped young dock leaves
4 scallions, chopped
2 cups (500 mL) all-purpose flour
1 cup (250 mL) cornmeal
2 tsp. (10 mL) baking powder
1/4 cup (60 mL) grated Parmesan cheese
1/2 cup (125 mL) canned chickpeas, drained
3 large eggs
1 1/4 cup (300 mL) milk
3 tbsp. (45 mL) melted butter

Melt butter in a skillet over medium heat. Add dock leaves and scallions and cook until tender, about 10 minutes. Remove from heat and set aside. Combine flour, cornmeal, baking powder and cheese together in a large bowl. In a medium bowl, combine chickpeas, eggs, milk, butter and dock leaves mixture. Add to dry ingredients and blend. Pour into lined muffin tins. Bake in 375°F (190°C) oven for about 15 to 20 minutes. Makes 18 muffins.

Dock Quiche

I always buy my pie shells for this recipe.

2 (9", 23 cm) pie shells
1 lb. (454 g) chopped cooked bacon or ham
1 1/2 large onions, finely chopped
4 large eggs
2 cups (500 mL) milk
1/8 tsp. (0.5 mL) ground nutmeg
1/8 tsp. (0.5 mL) pepper
1 tsp. (5 mL) baking powder
1/2 cup (125 mL) flour
1 cup (250 mL) chopped dock leaves
1 1/2 cups (375 mL) extra-old cheddar cheese or Swiss cheese
1/2 cup (125 mL) extra-old cheddar cheese or Swiss cheese

Bake pie shells in 375°F (190°C) oven for about 5 to 7 minutes. Set aside to cool.

Cook bacon and transfer to a paper towel to drain. Clean pan, reserving 2 tbsp. (30 mL) fat. Fry onions in bacon fat over medium heat. Transfer onions to a paper towel to drain.

Combine eggs, milk and spices together in a large bowl, mixing well. Stir in next 4 ingredients and pour into cooled pie shells. Sprinkle tops with remaining cheese and bake in 350°F (175°C) oven for 50 to 55 minutes. To help prevent collapsing, when the quiches are finished baking, turn off oven and let them sit in oven with door open for about 5 minutes. Makes 2 quiches. Each quiche cuts into 4 servings.

Prickly Pear Cactus

Opuntia polyacantha

This plant grows on hilltops, in dry prairies and in sandy, light-textured soils. Prickly pear cactus varies a great deal in height, from well under 30 cm to 2 m (1 to 7'), depending upon the growth conditions and location. It often forms in clumps or

shrub-like mounds in the Prairies. Though the sections of the stem are often thought of as leaves, these sections are actually modified stems that can reach a length of 5 to 15 cm (2 to 6"). Stem sections remain green and are covered with spines up to 7 cm (2 3/4") long. The spines are located in the numerous areoles along the plant. In mid-summer, the plant produces a bright yellow flower, which grows into a sweet armour-free fruit.

86

Food

Used as a vegetable by plains Indigenous peoples and introduced to Europeans, the prickly pear is now a major crop in Sicily and parts of Spain. The spines are difficult to remove but can be separated from the plant by peeling, scorching or cutting them off. The pulp is similar in texture and flavour to okra and is very tasty when battered and deep-fried. The fruit is best eaten fresh.

Other Uses

Traditionally, cactus was planted around the pole bases of food-drying structures to protect the food from rodents. The sticky stems of the plant can be used to clarify water. The pulp has been used as a fixative for dyes and paint.

Baked Cactus with Cheese

1 lb. (454 g) cactus stems
1 tbsp. (15 mL) lemon juice
1/4 cup (60 mL) cheddar cheese

Peel cactus stems, removing any spines, and rinse. Place in a casserole dish, pour lemon juice over top and sprinkle with cheese. Bake in 350°F (175°C) oven for 8 to 10 minutes. Makes 4 servings.

Cactus Jelly

3 1/2 cups (875 mL) cactus fruit
1 (2 oz., 57 g) package of pectin
6 cups (1.5 L) granulated sugar
1 1/2 tbsp. (22 mL) lemon juice

Chop cactus fruit and place in a saucepan. Cover with water and boil for 15 minutes. Drain water and mash cactus. Strain through a cheese-cloth. Pour cactus juice back into saucepan and add remaining ingredients. Bring to a slow boil over medium-low heat until mixture thickens. Pour into in sterilized jars. Store in a cool, dark place for up to 3 months. Makes 4 cups (1 L).

Prickly pear cactus flower

Fireweed

Epilobium angustifolium

This plant grows in a wide variety of habitats, including moist meadows and open clearings. In boreal forest areas, as the common name suggests, the plant is frequently found in post-burn sites. It grows from 1 to 3 m (3 to 10') in height and has lance-shaped leaves growing along the stem. Fireweed has a very showy flower with a pink spike that blooms for several months in summer. The flowers have 4 petals that form narrow pods, which produce a large number of parachuted seeds that are released in fall.

Food

Fireweed shoots can be used in lieu of asparagus in most recipes, cooked on their own or mixed with other vegetables in salads, soups or any dish that calls for cooked greens. If you are lucky enough to harvest an abundance of fireweed shoots, blanch and freeze them for winter.

Medicine

Tea made from the leaves was used to treat coughs and asthma. The roots were peeled and applied as a poultice to burns, sores and rashes.

Curried Fireweed Shoots

1 1/4 cups (300 mL) lightly salted water
1 cup (250 mL) chopped young fireweed shoots
3 tbsp. (45 mL) butter
2 tbsp. (30 mL) plain flour
1 garlic clove, minced
1/4 tsp. (1 mL) sea salt
1/2 tsp. (2 mL) paprika

1 tsp. (5 mL) coriander seeds
1 tsp. (5 mL) cumin seeds
1 tbsp. (15 mL) curry powder
1 tsp. (5 mL) grated ginger root
1 2/3 cups (400 mL) coconut milk
2 hard-boiled eggs, sliced

Bring salted water to a boil. Add fire-weed shoots and simmer for about 10 minutes, until tender. Strain and set aside.

Melt butter in a frying pan over medium. Sprinkle flour over top and stir to form a roux. Add garlic, salt, paprika, coriander, cumin, curry powder and ginger root. Cook for 2 minutes, stirring constantly. Whisk in coconut milk until smooth. Bring to a boil and cook until well thickened. Arrange boiled fireweed on a serving plate, pour curry sauce over top and garnish with sliced eggs. Makes 4 servings.

Cream of Fireweed Soup

2 tbsp. (30 mL) butter
2 tbsp. (30 mL) flour
1 cup (250 mL) cream
1 cup (250 mL) chicken stock
1 cup (250 mL) chopped young fireweed shoots
1 tbsp. (15 mL) lemon juice
1 garlic clove, minced
Salt, to taste
Pepper, to taste

Melt butter in a saucepan over medium. Add flour and stir until smooth. Add cream, chicken stock, fireweed, lemon juice and garlic. Bring to a boil. Remove from heat and set aside to cool slightly. Puree mixture and season with salt and pepper. Makes 5 servings.

Fireweed Jelly

8 cups (2 L) fireweed blossoms, stems removed
1/4 cup (60 mL) lemon juice
4 1/2 cups (1.1 L) water
1 (2 oz., 57 g) package of pectin
5 cups (1.25 L) granulated sugar

Combine first 3 ingredients in a medium pot over medium. Bring to a boil and cook for 10 minutes. Strain and return liquid to pot. Heat over medium until lukewarm. Add pectin and bring to boil. Add sugar and cook at a full boil for about 20 minutes. Pour into sterilized jars and seal. Process sealed jars in a boiling water bath for 10 minutes. Makes 6 cups (1.5 L).

Fireweed Ice Cream

Use only the petals for this recipe, no stem or stamens.

2 cups (500 mL) heavy or whipping cream
1 cup (250 mL) milk
1 1/2 cups (375 mL) fireweed petals
2 large eggs yolks
3/4 cup (175 mL) fine sugar
2 tsp. (10 mL) honey

Combine cream, milk and petals in a saucepan and heat to just below boiling. Remove from heat, cover and set aside for 25 minutes to allow flavours to blend. Whisk egg yolks in a large mixing bowl until light and fluffy, about 1 to 2 minutes. Add sugar and honey to egg mixture a little at a time and continue whisking until completely blended. Strain milk mixture into egg mixture and return to saucepan or a double-boiler. Cook over low until slightly thickened, but do not let it boil. Chill custard mixture and freeze, or continue to process in an ice cream maker. Store in freezer. Makes 4 servings.

Flax

Linum usitatissimum

Flax in flower - the small green pods are immature seed capsules

This plant is cultivated in fields and grows wild along roadsides to a height of 30 cm (1'). Flax has long narrow leaves and fibrous stalks, and it produces round seedpods.

It is a perennial herb, blooming from May to August. The flowers are blue and have 5 petals. At least 2 wild flax species grow on the Prairies, including wild blue flax *(L. lewisii)* and yellow flax *(L. rigidum)*.

Food

Its oily seeds can be used in baked goods.

Medicine

Flax contains essential fatty acids, which are good for managing cholesterol levels.

Other Uses

The stalk is extremely fibrous. Throughout the centuries, people have beaten or threshed flax to make linen from the fibres. Fibres taken from the plant is two to three times as strong as those from cotton. Flax fibres were commonly used for vegetable-based cloth up until the 19th century, when cotton became more popular. Linen textiles appear to be some of the oldest in the world. Fragments dating back to about 8000 BCE have been found that contain flax mixtures of straw, seeds, fibres, yarns and various types of fabrics.

For nearly 1000 years, a variety of ancient Mediterranean civilizations used linen armour. Alexander the Great and his soldiers used linothorax, a lightweight yet effective body armour that protected the body but allowed freedom of movement. Whereas most ancient armour was made of metal, linothorax was produced by laminating together multiple layers of linen with available glues. Because of the perishable nature of the material, no examples have survived from the ancient world and linothorax remains a mystery; however, historians have recently made effective recreations of this armour.

Flax Crackers

1/4 cup (60 mL) flax seeds
1/4 cup (60 mL) ground flax seeds
1 1/2 cups (375 mL) all-purpose flour
1/2 tsp. (2 mL) baking powder
1/2 tsp. (2 mL) salt
4 tsp. (20 mL) softened butter
1/2 cup (125 mL) milk

Combine first 5 ingredients in a large bowl. Blend in butter. Add milk and stir until batter becomes doughy. Chill dough for about 10 minutes. On a lightly floured surface, roll out dough to 1.5 mm (1/16") thickness. Cut into 2 1/2" (6.5 cm) squares and place on an ungreased cookie sheet. Bake in 325°F (160°C) oven for about 20 minutes. Makes 24 crackers.

Flax Cookies

1 1/3 cups (325 mL) butter
1 1/4 cups (300 mL) granulated sugar
1 1/2 cups (375 mL) brown sugar, lightly packed
2 1/3 cups (575 mL) flax seeds
3 large eggs
1 1/2 tsp. (7 mL) vanilla
3 1/2 cups (875 mL) all-purpose flour
1 1/2 cups (375 mL) oatmeal
1 1/2 cups (375 mL) wheat germ

Cream together butter and sugars in a large bowl. Add flax seeds. In a separate bowl, combine eggs and vanilla. Add to butter mixture. Stir in remaining 3 ingredients. Roll dough into a log and refrigerate for 5 minutes. Cut into 1/4" (6 mm) slices. Bake in 350°F (175°C) oven for 12 to 15 minutes. Makes 24 cookies.

Flax Cookies

91

Wild sarsaparilla in flower

Wild Sarsaparilla

Aralia nudicaulis

Wild sarsaparilla is a perennial usually found growing in the understorey in wooded areas on the Prairies. The plant grows up to 1 m (3') in height. Its leaves are oval shaped with pointed ends; the flowers are whitish green. Sarsaparilla fruit forms a ball-shaped cluster and is inedible.

Food

Dried and ground sarsaparilla root is used in teas and root beer. Traditionally, chewing the root was thought to increase energy, and Indigenous peoples chewed it before battles and brought it along on hunting expeditions.

Medicine

Wild sarsaparilla roots have been used as a treatment for upset stomach, sore throat, teething sickness and infections in wounds. There were also sometimes mixed with other herbs and used as a poultice.

Root Beer

If you don't have a vanilla bean, use 2 tsp. (10 mL) of vanilla extract instead and add it with the honey and sugar.

3 tbsp. (45 mL) sarsaparilla root, finely chopped
5 tbsp. (75 mL) sassafras
3 cardamom seedpods
1 (6", 15 cm) vanilla bean, cut into many small segments
4 black peppercorns
4 whole allspice
18 cups (4.5 L) water
1 tbsp. (15 mL) honey
2 cups (500 mL) granulated sugar
1/8 tsp. (0.5 mL) ale yeast

Place sarsaparilla, sassafras, cardamom, vanilla bean, peppercorns and allspice into a spice bag. Place spice bag in a stockpot with water, bring to a boil and then simmer for 30 minutes. Remove from heat and set aside to steep for 30 minutes. Remove spice bag. Stir in honey and sugar until dissolved. Let cool to 90°F (32°C).

Scoop a small amount of brewing water into a small glass. Add yeast to glass and let sit for 5 to 10 minutes to activate yeast. Meanwhile, strain brew into another vessel. Stir in yeast and bottle. Remember to stir your brew as you bottle it to ensure an even distribution of yeast. Use sterilized bottles that can withstand some pressure, such as beer bottles or plastic pop bottles.

Let your brew sit for several days to weeks after bottling for carbonation to begin. Allow more time for cooler climates, less time for hotter climates. Once carbonation is well underway, store in a cool place, or better yet, in the refrigerator, to limit excessive carbonation and a risk of exploding bottles. Makes about 18 cups (4.5 L).

WARNING: Plastic pop bottles work best for bottling because you can gauge the level of carbonation in the bottles by giving them a squeeze; when the bottles are firm, carbonation is well underway. Also, plastic bottles are less likely to explode under pressure from carbonation in comparison to glass. Because of this explosion hazard, I have always used plastic bottles for making root beer.

Lamb's Quarters

Chenopodium album

Also called: fat-hen, goosefoot, pigweed

This weedy plant favours waste grounds and disturbed areas but can be found in a wide variety of locations. The leaves are alternate and varied in appearance; the first leaves, nearest the base, are toothed and somewhat diamond shaped, whereas the second leaves, nearer the upper stem, have a smooth, lanceolate shape with a whitish, waxy coating on the underside. Lamb's quarters generally grows upright to a varying height of about 10 cm to 1.5 m (4" to 5'). When in flower, the plant sometimes tends to a recumbent or laying-down posture because of the weight of the seeds and covering foliage. The flowers themselves are small and symmetrical; they grow in small cymes on a densely branched inflorescence.

Food

Although considered a weed in many regions, lamb's quarters is cultivated in some areas as a vegetable similar to spinach, as well as for its seed, which can be used as a dietary grain or cereal. Try using lamb's quarters in place of spinach in a salad, and drizzle with raspberry vinegar for a dressing.

94

Lamb's Quarters Breakfast

1 cup (250 mL) lamb's quarters leaves
4 bacon strips, chopped
1 tbsp. (15 mL) butter
1 medium onion, chopped
1 tbsp. (15 mL) balsamic vinegar
1/4 cup (60 mL) water
2 eggs
2 tbsp. (30 mL) grated Parmesan
   cheese

Remove and wash leaves from stems of lamb's quarters.

Cook bacon in a medium frying pan until crispy. Transfer to a paper towel to drain.

Heat butter in a separate pan over medium. Add onion and cook until trans-lucent. Add vinegar, water and lamb's quarters. Cover and cook on low heat for 5 minutes. Stir in bacon. Spoon mixture into 2 ramekin dishes, crack an egg over each and sprinkle Parmesan over top. Bake in 350°F (175°C) oven for 20 min-utes. If you prefer a softer egg, shorten the cooking time. Makes 2 servings.

Lamb's Quarter Pesto

1 cup (250 mL) spinach
1/2 cup (125 mL) green onions
1 carrot, finely grated
1/2 cup (125 mL) grated Parmesan
1/2 cup (125 mL) chopped olives
4 cups (1 L) fresh lamb's quarters
   leaves
1/2 cup (125 mL) olive oil
4 garlic cloves
1/2 cup (125 mL) pecans
Salt, to taste
1/4 tsp. (1 mL) pepper

Chop spinach and cook in a frying pan over medium until tender. Drain and transfer to a blender. In a medium saucepan, cook green onions, carrot, cheese and olives over medium.

Let cool and transfer to blender with spinach. Blend spinach, lamb's quarters, olive oil, garlic, pecans, salt and pepper until it forms a smooth paste. Store in refrigerator for up to 3 weeks. Makes 8 1/2 cups (2.1 L).

Lamb's Quarters Frittata

6 large eggs
1/3 cup (75 mL) grated Parmesan
   or Romano cheese
Salt, to taste
Pepper, to taste
1 tbsp. (15 mL) butter
1 small onion
5 strips bacon, roughly chopped
1/4 lb. (113 g) lamb's quarters, tough
   stems removed

In a medium bowl, whisk together eggs, cheese, salt and pepper. Set aside.

Heat butter in a 12" oven-safe skillet over medium and cook onions until translucent. Add bacon and cook until almost crispy. Add lamb's quarters and cook until wilted. Spread mixture evenly across skillet and pour egg mixture over top, smoothing evenly with a spatula. Bake in 350°F (175°C) oven for 8 to 10 minutes, until bottom has set and frittata is just beginning to set on top, then broil for 3 or 4 minutes, until top is golden brown. Makes 5 servings.

Cream of Lamb's Quarters Soup

1/4 cup (60 mL) butter
1 onion, finely chopped
1/4 tsp. (1 mL) ground nutmeg
1/4 cup (60 mL) flour
4 cups (1 L) homemade chicken stock
3 1/2 cups (875 mL) young lamb's quarters leaves
Juice from 1/2 lemon
1 cup (250 mL) whipping cream
Salt, to taste
Pepper, to taste
Croutons, for garnish
Toasted pumpkin seeds, for garnish

Heat butter in a heavy-bottomed medium pot over medium-low and cook onions until lightly browned. Add nutmeg. Add flour and stir constantly to make a roux. Slowly add chicken stock, whisking constantly to prevent flour from clumping. Simmer, stirring frequently, until thickened, about 10 minutes. Add lamb's quarters and cook until tender, about 5 minutes. Stir in lemon juice to preserve colour. Remove from heat and cool slightly before transferring to blender. Purée until smooth. Return soup to saucepan over medium heat and add cream. Season with salt and pepper. Serve topped with croutons and toasted pumpkin seeds. Makes 5 servings.

Lamb's Quarters Soup

1 tbsp. (15 mL) butter
1 medium onion, finely chopped
2 garlic cloves
1 cup (250 mL) cashews
1 ripe tomato
1 1/2 cups (375 mL) chicken stock
Juice from 1/2 lime
1 tbsp. (15 mL) olive oil
1 tsp. (5 mL) honey
Sea salt, to taste
1 cup (250 mL) freshly picked lamb's quarters, chopped
1/2 medium avocado cut into cubes
1/2 red bell pepper sliced in thin strips

Heat butter in a medium frying pan over medium. Add onions and garlic and cook until golden brown. Transfer to a blender and add remaining ingredients. Puree until smooth. Pour mixture into a saucepot, bring to a boil and serve. Makes 5 servings.

Lamb's Quarters Couscous Warm Salad

1 cup (250 mL) plain yogurt
1 cup (250 mL) couscous
1 1/2 cups (375 mL) lamb's quarters
1 tsp. (5 mL) cumin seed
2 tbsp. (30 mL) olive oil
2 large garlic cloves, smashed and chopped
1 jalapeño pepper
Salt, to taste
1/2 cup (125 mL) chicken stock
2 tbsp. (30 mL) extra-virgin olive oil
1/3 cup (75 mL) roasted pistachios, chopped
1/4 cup (60 mL) raisins
1 tsp. (5 mL) chopped mint

Drain yogurt for 30 minutes using layers of cheesecloth, and discard liquid. Transfer thickened yogurt to a bowl and set aside.

Cook couscous according to package directions. Drain and set aside.

Wash lamb's quarters in cool water, pat dry and strip leaves from stems. Toast cumin seeds in a small skillet over medium-low until fragrant. Set aside to cool. Use a mortar and pestle to grind seeds into powder.

In a large, heavy skillet, heat olive oil over medium. Add garlic and jalapeño, stirring regularly until garlic is golden and jalapeño is lightly toasted. Add cumin, lamb's quarters, salt and chicken stock. Reduce heat to medium-low and cook, stirring occasionally, until lamb's quarters is wilted and tender. Stir in couscous, increasing heat if necessary to reduce any remaining liquid. Remove pan from heat, and drizzle mixture with extra-virgin olive oil. Add pistachios, raisins and mint. Mix well. Serve warm, garnished with yogurt. Makes 4 servings.

Sweetgrass

Hierochloe odorata

Also called: Seneca grass, holy grass and vanilla grass

Sweetgrass is a sacred plant for the Indigenous peoples of the plains and prairies of North America. It is a tall, wild grass with a reddish base, growing to a height of 30 to 60 cm (1 to 2'). Its sweet fragrance can help identify the grass, which has a vanilla or tobacco scent. Once found growing abundantly across the Prairies, sweetgrass is uncommon today, as much of its habitat has been changed or destroyed by encroaching development and cultivation.

Medicine

Tea made from the plant has been used to treat colds, fevers, coughs and sore throats. Cooled tea has been used as a wash for treating wind burns and sore eyes.

Other Uses

Sweetgrass is braided in bunches and burned during sacred ceremonies. Indigenous peoples believe burning sweetgrass and sage will bring good spirits and pure thoughts.

Asparagus emerging

Asparagus shoots

Wild Asparagus
Asparagus officinalis

This herbaceous, perennial plant species is in the genus *Asparagus*. At one time, similar to the *Allium* (onion) relatives garlic and onion, asparagus was considered part of the lily family. However, the Liliaceae classification has since been split, placing asparagus into the family Asparagaceae. Generally found growing by roadsides and riverbanks, wild asparagus can reach a height of 100 to 150 cm (3 to 5'). It has stout stems, with emerging spears that develop into many-branched, feathery foliage with needle-like cladodes (modified stems) in the axils of scale leaves. The greenish-white or yellow flowers are bell shaped with 6 tepals partially fused at the base. Flowers are produced singly or in clusters of 2 or 3 along the junctions of the branchlets. Asparagus is usually dioecious, with male and female flowers on separate plants. The fruit consists of small red berries, 6 to 12 mm (1/4 to 1/2") diameter, with tiny black seeds inside. **The berries are poisonous to humans.**

Food
Wild asparagus is a green vegetable, edible (except for the berries) both raw and cooked. It can take the place of store-bought asparagus in recipes.

Medicine
Traditionally the spears were used to treat muscle spasms and rheumatism.

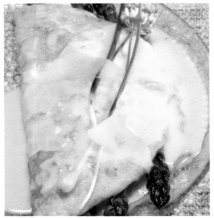

Asparagus Omelette with wild onions

Asparagus Omelette

This is one of my favourite recipes. It is especially good with Wild Onion Cheese Sauce (p. 108) poured overtop.

6 asparagus spears
2 eggs
1 tbsp. (15 mL) water
1 tbsp. (15 mL) butter

Pan sear asparagus spears (see below). Blend eggs and water thoroughly. Melt butter in a medium pan over medium. Add egg mixture and cook each side until light golden brown, about 1 1/2 minutes per side. Remove from pan and fold omelette over asparagus. Makes 2 servings.

Pan Seared Asparagus

For extra flavour sprinkle grated Parmesan cheese overtop before serving.

10 to 12 asparagus spears
1 tbsp. (15 mL) butter
1 tsp. (5 mL) lemon juice

Break tops off asparagus and set aside. Cut spears into about 1" (2.5 cm) lengths. Heat butter in a large frying pan over medium. Add spears and cook until almost tender. Add tops and cook until tender. Drizzle with lemon juice. Makes 6 servings.

Asparagus Soup

1 tbsp. (15 mL) butter
2 tbsp. (30 mL) flour
1 cup (250 mL) milk
1/8 tsp. (0.5 mL) ground nutmeg
1/8 tsp. (0.5 mL) pepper
25 asparagus spears
1 cup (250 mL) chicken stock

Melt butter in a medium saucepan over medium. Stir in flour to make a roux. Slowly add milk, whisking constantly, until mixture thickens into a white sauce. Add in spices.

Steam asparagus stalks, setting tips aside. Puree chicken stock and asparagus in a blender. Add mixture to white sauce in saucepan. Stir in asparagus tops and simmer for 5 to 7 minutes. Makes 6 servings.

Bacon-wrapped Asparagus

If your bacon is thick, you may want to cook it a little before wrapping the asparagus spears; prosciutto will most likely not need additional cooking.

8 asparagus spears
8 bacon or prosciutto slices

Snap woody ends off asparagus where the spears break naturally and discard ends. If asparagus is tough, peel thicker bases of spears to make them tender. Wrap a slice of bacon or prosciutto around each spear, leaving tips exposed. Place wrapped spears on a grill pan so fat can drip off. Bake in 400°F (200°C) oven for 15 to 20 minutes until bacon or prosciutto is crispy. Makes 8 pieces.

Raw Asparagus Salad with Parmesan Dressing

Add a poached egg per person to make this a delicious breakfast dish.

2 lbs. (900 g) asparagus
3 tbsp. (45 mL) lemon juice
2 tbsp. (30 mL) warm water
1/4 cup (60 mL) olive oil
1 cup (250 mL) grated Parmesan
   cheese
Salt, to taste
Pepper, to taste

Snap ends off asparagus where the spears break naturally and discard woody ends. Peel asparagus spears into shaved strips and place into a bowl. Set aside.

In a separate bowl, whisk together lemon juice, water, olive oil and Parmesan. Pour dressing over asparagus and toss gently, making sure to coat spears evenly. Season with salt and pepper, and serve. Makes 5 servings.

Asparagus Quiche

I always buy my pie shells for this recipe.

1 lb. (454 g) bacon, chopped
1 1/2 large onions, finely chopped
20 asparagus spears
4 large eggs
2 cups (500 mL) milk
1/8 tsp. (0.5 mL) ground nutmeg
1/8 tsp. (0.5 mL) pepper
1 1/4 cups (300 mL) grated extra-old
   cheddar or Swiss cheese
1 tsp. (5 mL) baking powder
1/2 cup (125 mL) flour
2 (9", 23 cm) pre-baked pie shells
1/4 cup (60 mL) grated cheddar or
   Swiss cheese

In a large frying pan, cook bacon over medium-high. Remove to a paper towel and reserve fat in pan. In another large pan, fry onions in 2 tbsp. (30 mL) reserved fat. Transfer cooked onions to paper towel with bacon to drain and cool.

Chop asparagus stalks into 1" (2.5 cm) lengths. Set aside, keeping the tips separate for later decoration. Place eggs, milk and spices in a large bowl and blend well. Stir in next 3 ingredients. Divide mixture between both pie shells and top with tips and remaining cheese. Bake in 350°F (175°C) oven for 50 to 55 minutes until centre has set. Let quiches stand in oven for about 5 minutes with door open so they do not collapse. Makes 2 quiches. Each quiche cuts into 4 servings.

Asparagus Quiche

Western Red Lily

Lilium philadelphicum

Tiger lily in flower

This showy flower is widely distributed across the Prairies and elsewhere in North America, growing in moist meadows, open woodland, prairies and occasionally in ditches. The lily grows to a height of approximately 30 to 90 cm (1 to 3'). Between June and August, the plant produces red or orange flowers covered in spots. The narrow, linear leaves alternate on the lower stem and are whorled on the upper stem.

As this plant may be protected in some regions, it is best to check its status before considering harvest. In Saskatchewan, the western red lily, or red wood lily *(L. philadelphicum* var. *andinum)* is the official provincial flower and is listed as a rare and protected species. The eastern red wood lily *(L. philadelphicum* var. *philadelphicum)* is also listed as a rare species in Saskatchewan. These species are not listed in Alberta or Manitoba, according to a recent provincial database search. I have a substantial population of edible wood lily cultivars in my garden and have controlled their expansion by using them for cooking.

Food

Indigenous peoples have used the bulb of the western red lily in soup and stews, like a potato. The unopened flower buds have also been used as food. The edible flower buds of cultivated varieties are used in cooking, particularly across Asia. They add flavour to Chinese dishes, egg recipes and salads.

Medicine

A tincture made from the plant has been used to treat nausea in pregnancy as well as congestion.

Vegan Hot and Sour Soup

2 tbsp. (30 mL) dried wood ear mushroom

4 dried shiitake mushrooms

12 dried tiger lily buds

1 1/2 cups (375 mL) hot water

2 tsp. (10 mL) bamboo fungus

1/4 cup (60 mL) lightly salted hot water

3 tbsp. (45 mL) soy sauce

3 tbsp. (45 mL) rice vinegar

1 tbsp. (15 mL) cornstarch

1 (8 oz., 225 g) container of firm tofu, cut into 1/4" (6 mm) strips

4 cups (1 L) vegetable broth

1/4 tsp. (1 mL) dried crushed chilies

1/2 tsp. (2 mL) pepper

3/4 tsp. (4 mL) ground white pepper

3 tbsp. (45 mL) cornstarch

1 tbsp. (15 mL) water

1/2 tbsp. (7 mL) chili oil

1/2 tbsp. (7 mL) sesame oil

1 green onion, thinly sliced

Combine wood ear mushrooms, shiitake mushrooms, lily buds and hot water in a small bowl. Soak for 20 minutes, until rehydrated. Drain, reserving liquid. Trim stems from mushrooms and cut mushrooms into thin strips. Cut lily buds in half.

In a separate bowl, soak bamboo fungus in lightly salted hot water. Soak about 20 minutes, until rehydrated. Drain and mince fungus, reserving liquid.

In a separate small bowl, combine soy sauce, rice vinegar and first amount of cornstarch. Add half of tofu strips. In a medium saucepan, mix reserved mushroom and lily bud liquid with vegetable broth. Bring to a boil. Stir in mushrooms and lily buds. Reduce heat and simmer for 3 to 5 minutes. Season with dried crushed chilies, pepper and white pepper.

In another small bowl, combine remaining cornstarch and water. Stir into broth mixture and cook until thickened. Add tofu in soy sauce mixture and remaining tofu strips to saucepan. Return to a boil and stir in bamboo fungus, chili oil and sesame oil. Garnish with green onions and serve. Makes 5 servings.

Lily Bulb Soup

10 asparagus spears
1 tsp. (5 mL) cooking oil
1 garlic clove, smashed
2 shallots, sliced
1 cup (250 mL) of chicken stock
4 lily bulbs, peeled
Sesame oil, to taste
Salt, to taste
Pepper, to taste
Chopped cilantro, for garnish
Grated ginger root, for garnish

Cut tips off asparagus spears and set aside. Cut spears into 1" (2.5 cm) pieces and set aside. Heat oil in a saucepan over medium. Add garlic and shallots and cook until shallots are golden. Add chicken stock and bring to a boil. Add asparagus spears and lily bulbs and boil for another 5 minutes. Add sesame oil and asparagus tips and season with salt and pepper. Garnish with chopped cilantro and grated ginger root. Makes 5 servings.

Stir-Fried Snow Peas with Fresh Lily Bulbs

1 tbsp. (15 mL) olive oil
1/2 tsp. (2 mL) grated ginger root
1/4 lb. (113 g) snow peas, trimmed
2 fresh lily bulbs, trimmed and peeled
1 carrot, sliced thinly with a peeler
Salt, to taste
Pepper, to taste

Heat oil in a pan and sauté ginger root until fragrant. Add snow peas and stir-fry briskly for 30 seconds. Add lily bulbs and carrot slices to the pan and stir-fry for another 30 seconds. Season with salt and pepper. Makes 4 servings.

Lily Bulb Salad

2 lily bulbs
1 tbsp. (15 mL) olive oil
1 small sweet onion, sliced vertically and separated
2 whole wild onions, blanched
10 green asparagus spears, blanched and sliced lengthwise
10 white asparagus spears, blanched and sliced lengthwise
2 lily stems, sliced into long thin strips
1 tbsp. (15 mL) black bean vinaigrette (see below)
Chive flowers, for garnish
Pansies, for garnish

Peel lily bulbs into petals. Heat olive oil in a medium frying pan over medium and add lily petals. Cook until petals are crisp. Combine petals with sweet onion in a medium bowl. Layer with blanched wild onions, sliced green asparagus and sliced white asparagus. Top with sliced lily stems. Drizzle with black bean vinaigrette (see below). Garnish with chive flowers and pansies. Makes 5 servings.

Black Bean Vinaigrette

2 tbsp. (30 mL) minced shallots
1 tbsp. (15 mL) minced ginger root
2 tbsp. (30 mL) fermented black beans, rinsed and chopped
1/4 cup (60 mL) rice vinegar
1/2 cup (125 mL) olive oil
1/4 cup (60 mL) mirin

Combine all ingredients in a small bowl or glass jar. Store in refrigerator for up to 2 weeks. Makes 1 cup (250 mL).

Wild Prairie Onion

Allium textile

This perennial plant is usually found growing on hillsides with native grasses and forbs. The plant can grow to 50 cm (20") in height. It has sickle-shaped, tubular leaves that resemble grass, and it blooms from spring to early summer, usually from May to June. The flower heads have a white or slightly pinkish hue and form ball-like clusters consisting of several blooms. Wild onion has an edible bulb covered with a dense skin of brown fibres. Take care when harvesting wild onions to avoid a similar-looking plant called death camas *(Zigadenus venenosus)*, which is poisonous. I have never seen it, but it also grows in native grasslands. A good rule of thumb is if it smells like an onion, it is an onion; if it does not smell like an onion, it is not an onion and do not eat it! Make sure you bring your guidebook with you or seek the opinion of a knowledgeable person before you head out collecting. Also, avoid nodding onion *(A. cernuum)* in Saskatchewan, where it is listed as rare (it is not listed in Alberta or Manitoba, according to a recent search of provincial databases).

Food

Wild onions are harvestable as a root crop, similar to commercial onions. The flowers are also edible and are great in salads. Wild onions add flavour to soups and stews, and help to make the best cheese sauce for omelettes, one of my favourite dishes.

Medicine

The plant is reported to have antibacterial, antifungal and antiviral properties as a result of a complex mix of compounds that are active antimicrobials (MacKinnon et.al., 2014). Teas were made to treat colds, sore throats and coughs. The bulb of the onion placed directly on a wart has been used to help kill the virus.

Thanks to Swedish-born Carl Linnaeus (1707–98) and plants like the onion, we have an internationally used classification system for plants and animals. This classification system gives species precise names that show identification and relationship to other species through a system known as binomial nomenclature. This system was made possible in part because of confusion caused by the onion, one of the oldest of the cultivated vegetables and whose precise origin is uncertain. It seems that most cultures used it, and there were numerous names for the same plant and its varieties. By the time Linnaeus attended university in Uppsala, mariners were bringing in vast numbers of plant species from the New World. Bill Laws eloquently describes the resulting botanical confusion in his book *Fifty Plants that Changed the Course of History:* "In the ensuing horticultural confusion, some plants acquired several names, making the task of systematically giving them each a scientific name something of a nightmare." (Laws, 2012: 11). Linnaeus and a fellow student, Peter Artedi, set out to make order of the natural world by classifying plants and animals. Unfortunately, Artedi died in 1735, but Linnaeus continued the work.

By the 1700s botanists and naturalists agreed that similar plants could be placed in family groups, such as grouping onions, leeks and garlic in the lily family. Linnaeus took a further step, consistently subdividing families into genera and then into precise species, based on specific observable characteristics. For the numerous onion species, Linnaeus took the genus as a first name and the species as the second name and subsequently classified many onion species, settling the tearful confusion. He did this by analyzing features such as the number of stamens and stigmas on the plant and using a sexual system of classification that is still used today.

Wild Onion Cheese Sauce

This sauce is fabulous on asparagus omelettes. See p. 100 for a photo of an asparagus omelette with this sauce.

2 tbsp. (30 mL) butter
2 tbsp. (30 mL) flour
1 1/4 cup (300 mL) milk
10 wild onion bulbs and flower heads
1 cup (250 mL) aged cheddar
Pepper, to taste

Melt butter in a saucepan over medium. Add flour and slowly add milk, stirring constantly until mixture thickens, about 10 minutes. Add onions and cheese and stir until cheese is melted. Season with pepper. Makes 1 1/4 cups (300 mL).

Macaroni and Cheese with Crab

1 1/4 cups (300 mL) Wild Onion
    Cheese Sauce (see above)
1/4 cup (60 mL) crab meat
1 cup (250 mL) macaroni
1/2 cup (125 mL) grated extra
    old cheddar cheese

Combine sauce and crab in a large bowl. Cook pasta according to package directions. Drain and add to bowl with crab mixture, stirring to combine. Pour mixture into a buttered baking dish and sprinkle with cheese. Bake in 350°F (175°C) oven for 20 to 25 minutes, until cheese on top has melted and is golden. Makes 5 servings.

Pickled Wild Onions with Rosemary and Honey

You can also use pearl onions that have been blanched, peeled and trimmed for this recipe.

1 1/2 cups (375 mL) of small wild
    onions, trimmed
3 rosemary sprigs
1/2 cup (125 mL) white wine
    or Champagne vinegar
1/2 cup (125 mL) honey
    (local if possible)
1/4 cup (60 L) water
2 tbsp. (30 mL) fresh lemon juice
5 whole black peppercorns
1/4 tsp. (1 mL) salt
3 rosemary sprigs

Pack onions into 3 heatproof 1 cup (250 mL) glass jars, each about half full. Add 1 rosemary sprig to each jar. In a medium saucepan, combine vinegar, honey, water, lemon juice, peppercorns, salt and remaining rosemary sprigs and bring to a boil. Pour hot liquid over onions and place a small plate on top of each jar to keep them submerged. Let cool completely. Serve right away at room temperature, or refrigerate for up to 1 week. Makes 3 cups (750 mL).

Chicken and Mushrooms with Wild Onions

You can find dried wood ear mushrooms at Asian markets. This dish is great served over wild rice.

4 dried wood ear mushrooms
2 tbsp. (30 mL) olive oil
1 chicken, cut into pieces, skin-on
2 garlic cloves, crushed
2 rosemary sprigs
2 sprigs thyme
1/2 cup (125 mL) brown mushrooms, halved
1 1/3 (325 mL) cups pumpkin, peeled and chopped into 3/4" (2 cm) chunks
2 cups (500 mL) chicken stock
2 tbsp. (30 mL) roughly chopped wild onions
Salt, to taste
Pepper, to taste
1 tbsp. (15 mL) butter
1 cup (250 mL) cooked wild rice

Soak wood ear mushrooms in hot water for 15 to 20 minutes to rehydrate, then drain and slice into strips.

Heat olive oil in a heavy-based, oven-proof casserole dish over medium. Add chicken pieces and sear for 3 to 4 minutes on all sides, until golden brown all over. Add garlic, rosemary, thyme and brown mushrooms and cook for 1 to 2 minutes. Add pumpkin and enough stock to cover ingredients halfway. Set remaining stock aside. Cook chicken mixture, covered, in 350°F (175°C) oven for about 40 minutes, until chicken is cooked through. Transfer chicken to a warm plate, cover with foil and set aside to rest. Return casserole dish to heat and bring to a simmer. Add wild onions and cook until tender. Season with salt and pepper.

In a separate pan, heat butter and 6 tbsp. (90 ml) of reserved chicken stock. Add wood ear mushrooms and gently braise until tender. To serve, place chicken on cooked wild rice, pour wild onion sauce over top and garnish with wood ear mushrooms. Makes 5 servings.

Scarlet Mallow

Sphaeralcea coccinea

A widespread, low-growing plant common on the dry prairie, scarlet mallow grows in fields, along roadsides and in disturbed areas. The plant usually grows from to 10 to 30 cm (4" to 1') in height. It has greyish-green, lobed, alternating leaves with silver hairs, and bright orange flowers that bloom from July to September. The fruit of the scarlet mallow is a spherical capsule that has a nutty, cheese-like flavour when ripe.

Food
The seed is edible and can be used as a thickening agent. The root of some members of the mallow family is used to make marshmallows. The roots can be used to make a mild tea. The plant is high in vitamin A.

Medicine
A cool tea was used as a wash for skin issues such as cuts, rash and burns.

Milkweed

Asclepias spp.

The milkweeds vary in habitat preference, growing in dry soils, fields, on roadsides and in riparian areas. The umbel globular flowers of milkweeds also vary significantly in colour, from rosy red, to pale pink and purple, to greenish white. One of the more common species, showy milkweed *(A. speciosa)* grows up to 2 m (7') in height. Its leaves are oval and opposite of each other. The plant typically blooms in July, with clusters of pale pink, globular-shaped flowers, each floret having 5 petals. The flower heads become seedpods that open when ripe to release numerous silky parachute-like seeds. A few of the milkweed plant species are extremely rare, including silky milkweed *(A. syriaca)* and whorled milkweed *(A. verticillata)*. The monarch butterfly *(Danaus plexippus)*, a protected insect, requires milkweed; it consumes the nectar from the flowers and lays its eggs on the leaves. After they hatch, monarch caterpillars eat only milkweed plants. If you are planning to harvest milkweed, first check for any sign of monarchs and confirm that the milkweed is a common species.

Showy milkweed in flower

Food

The plant is edible but **must be cooked.** The young shoots and seedpods can be cooked like asparagus. The stalks can be blanched to remove their milky fluid.

WARNING: Milkweed is toxic if not cooked properly.

Medicine

The sap, which is sticky and milky, can be applied to burns, minor cuts, warts and rashes caused by poison ivy.

Milkweed Fritters

1 cup (250 mL) whole wheat flour
1/2 tsp. (2 mL) baking powder
1/2 tsp. (2 mL) salt
2 eggs
6 oz. (170 mL) beer
20 clusters of milkweed blossoms

Combine flour, baking powder and salt. Stir in eggs and beer. Let stand for 1 hour.

Bring a small pot of water to a boil. Blanch blossoms until they are bright green, approximately 1 minute. Heat fresh canola oil in a deep fryer to 325°F (160°C). Dip each flower blossom in batter. Make sure to fully cover whole surface. Drip off excess batter and deep fry in oil until golden brown. Makes about 12 fritters.

Milkweed Flower Quiche

5 large eggs
1/4 cup (60 mL) flour
1/2 tsp. (2 mL) baking powder
Salt, to taste
Pepper, to taste
1 cup (250 mL) cottage cheese
2 cups (500 mL) shredded cheddar cheese
1/4 cup (60 mL) olive oil
8 oz. (225 g) cooked milkweed flower buds

Whip eggs until frothy. Stir in remaining ingredients. Pour mixture into a greased 9 x 9" (23 x 23 cm) pan. Bake in 350°F (175°C) oven for 30 minutes, or until eggs are set and top is browned. Makes 6 servings.

Cream of Milkweed Flower Buds Soup

3 cups (750 mL) milkweed flower buds
1 tbsp. (15 mL) oil
2 tbsp. (30 mL) butter
1/2 small onion, diced
3 tbsp. (45 L) flour
2 cups (500 mL) milk
1/2 cup (125 mL) vegetable broth
1 medium russet potato, diced
1 cup (250 mL) shredded sharp cheddar

Steam milkweed flower buds for 7 to 10 minutes and set aside, keeping them warm.

Heat oil and butter in a medium frying pan over medium. Add onion and cook until translucent. Add flour and whisk for 30 seconds over medium-high heat. Slowly pour in milk and vegetable broth, whisking constantly to prevent lumps. Add potato and bring mixture to a boil. Reduce heat to medium and cook, stirring occasionally, until thickened. Cool slightly. Puree mixture in a blender with 2 1/2 cups (625 mL) steamed milkweed flower buds until smooth. Add cheese and stir until melted. Serve garnished with remaining steamed milkweed flower buds. Makes 5 servings.

Roasted Milkweed Shoots

1 lb. (454 g) milkweed shoots
2 tbsp. (30 mL) olive oil
2 garlic cloves, minced
Kosher salt, to taste
Pepper, to taste
2 prosciutto slices
1 lemon

Rinse shoots and place in a plastic bag. Add oil and rub bag so oil gets evenly distributed. Sprinkle with garlic, salt and pepper. Lay shoots out in a single layer in a baking dish or a foil-covered roasting pan. Cut prosciutto into 1/4" (6 mm) pieces and sprinkle over shoots. Cook in 400°F (200°C) oven for 8 to 10 minutes, until shoots are lightly browned and tender when pierced with a fork. Drizzle with fresh lemon juice before serving. Makes 4 servings.

Buffalo-Style Milkweed Pods

1 1/2 cups (375 mL) bread crumbs
1/4 cup (60 mL) flour
1 tbsp. (15 mL) garlic powder
1 tsp. (5 mL) paprika
1 tsp. (5 mL) oregano
1 tsp. (5 mL) cayenne
1 tsp. (5 mL) turmeric
1 egg
1/2 cup (125 mL) almond milk
1/2 cup (125 mL) water
20 young milkweed pods
Hot sauce, to taste
1 tbsp. (15 mL) wing sauce of your
   choice

Combine dry ingredients in a large bowl. In a separate bowl, combine egg, almond milk and water. Stir in dry ingredients. Dip milkweed pods into batter. Place on a baking sheet covered with parchment paper. Cook in 350°F (175°C) oven for 15 to 20 minutes, until crisp. Remove from oven and transfer to a large bowl. Add wing sauce and stir to evenly coat pods. Return pods to baking sheet cook for 10 minutes. Makes 5 servings.

Bergamot in flower

Bergamot

Monarda fistulosa

Also called: bee balm

Bergamot is a perennial herb that prefers sunny areas with moist or slightly dry soil. It usually grows about 50 cm to over 1 m (20" to 3') in height, with pointed, ovate leaves varying in colour from light to dark green. The flowers are pink or lavender and bloom in mid-summer.

Food

Use fresh or dried leaves to season tomato dishes and herb breads, and as a substitute for sage in stuffing for poultry and meats, especially pork and veal. Bergamot adds a sage-like flavour to roasts. It is best to use the flowers for teas; the leaves have a hotter, oregano-like flavor. Enliven the look and taste of salads by adding a sprinkling of bergamot flowers.

Medicine

The plant has been used in ointments to help soothe sore muscles. Bergamot tea is used to treat coughs, colds and sore throats.

114

Bergamot Rosehip Jelly

Gooseberry and Bergamot Jelly

1/2 cup (125 mL) chopped bergamot
leaves

8 cups (2 L) of gooseberries

2 cups (500 mL) water

3 1/2 cups (875 mL) granulated sugar

1 (2 oz., 57 g) package of pectin

Combine bergamot leaves, gooseberries
and water in a large pot. Bring to a boil.
Add sugar and pectin and stir to dissolve. Reduce heat and simmer for
10 minutes, until flavours have fully
blended. Strain juice using a fine-mesh
strainer and discard pulp. Pour into sterilized jars. Makes 6 cups (1.5 L).

Rosehip Bergamot Jelly

8 cups (2 L) rosehips

4 cups (1 L) apple juice

1/2 cup (125 mL) bergamot leaves and
flower petals

4 cups (1 L) granulated sugar

1 (2 oz., 57 g) package of pectin

In a large pot, combine rosehips and
apple juice and bring to a boil for
10 minutes. Strain out rosehips. Add
bergamot, sugar and pectin and stir to
dissolve. Reduce heat and simmer until
flavours have fully blended. Pour into
sterilized jars. Makes 6 cups (1.5 mL).

Lamb Shanks with Bergamot Sauce

1/4 cup (60 mL) flour

Salt, to taste

Pepper, to taste

1/2 tsp. (2 mL) finely chopped bergamot leaves

4 lamb shanks (about 4 lbs., 1.8 kg,
total)

1 cup (250 mL) homemade chicken
stock

1/4 cup (60 mL) balsamic vinegar

6 tbsp. (90 mL) rosehip bergamot jelly
(see this page)

1 tbsp. (15 mL) cornstarch

Season flour with salt, pepper and bergamot. Roll lamb shanks in mixture.
Grease a baking dish large enough to
accommodate lamb and sauce. Bake
lamb in 350°F (175°C) oven for 2 hours.

Combine next 3 ingredients in a saucepot and simmer so flavours blend.
Remove lamb from oven. Transfer lamb
to a plate and drain grease from baking
dish. Pour sauce into baking dish, stirring to get browning off bottom of dish
and blended into sauce. Place lamb
back in dish and bake for another
30 minutes.

In a small bowl, mix cornstarch and
4 tbsp. (60 mL) of sauce borrowed from
baking dish to make a roux. Remove
dish from oven and transfer lamb to
a plate. Pour roux into baking dish and
stir to thicken. Place lamb back in dish
and cook for another 10 minutes.
Remove from oven and let lamb rest
for a few minutes before serving. Makes
4 servings.

Chili Chicken Salad with Bergamot

1 lb. (454 g) boneless, skinless
  chicken breasts
1 orange, thinly sliced
1 lemon, thinly sliced
1 tsp. (5 mL) chili powder
1 tsp. (5 mL) ground cumin
Ground cloves, to taste
1 green onion, minced
1 shallot, minced
3 tbsp. (45 mL) minced fresh
  bergamot leaves
1/4 cup (60 mL) plain yogurt
1 tsp. (5 mL) fresh lemon juice
Flour tortillas or lettuce leaves
  for serving

Place chicken, orange and lemon slices
in a shallow frying pan. Fill with just
enough water to cover chicken, and
bring to a boil. Reduce heat to low and
simmer until chicken is cooked through,
about 20 minutes. Remove chicken to
a plate to cool. When it's cool enough
to handle, shred chicken into bite-sized
pieces.

In a small dry skillet, heat chili powder,
cumin and cloves over medium-high
until fragrant, about 1 1/2 minutes.
Transfer to a large bowl and stir in green
onions, shallot, bergamot, yogurt and
lemon juice. Add chicken and toss well
to combine. Serve at room temperature
or very slightly chilled, rolled up in tortillas or lettuce leaves. Makes 5 servings.

Bergamot Bread

*Use only the outer soft petals of the
bergamot flowers for this recipe. The
bread is best when allowed to rest in
the refrigerator overnight.*

1 (1/4 oz., 7 g) package active dry yeast
1/4 cup (60 mL) warm water
2 tbsp. (30 mL) butter
1/2 tsp. (2 mL) honey
4 cups (1 L) flour
1 cup (250 mL) bergamot flowers
1 cup (250 mL) water, room
  temperature
1 egg white, slightly beaten
1/4 cup (60 mL) bergamot flowers

Dissolve yeast in warm water in a small
mixing bowl or cup and set aside to
activate.

Combine butter and honey in a separate
bowl. Stir in flour and flower petals. Add
room temperature water and yeast mixture. Knead mixture into dough by hand.
Shape into a ball and place in a greased
bowl, turning once to oil all surfaces.
Cover with a damp towel; let stand in
a warm place until dough has doubled
in bulk. Punch dough down, turn it out
onto a lightly floured board and knead
for 5 minutes. Divide dough in half and
shape into 2 round loaves. Place loaves
about 10 cm (4") apart on a greased
cookie sheet and cover with a damp
towel. Set aside for 30 minutes to rise.
Brush top with beaten egg white. Dip
remaining bergamot blossoms in egg
white and spread over top of bread.
Bake loaves in 400°F (200°C) oven for
45 to 50 minutes, or until lightly
browned. Makes 2 loaves.

Young hyssop

Hyssop

Agastache foeniculum

This perennial herb grows up to 60 cm (2') in height in moist fertile soils in parkland areas. As a member of the mint family, hyssop has a square stem. The toothed, oval-shaped leaves culminate to a point, and the flowers are blue or violet spikes.

Food

Hyssop is a useful herb for flavouring soups, stews, salads and teas.

Medicine

Hyssop tea was used to treat colds, coughs and sore throats. A poultice made from the leaves was used to help heal bruises.

117

Hyssop Sauce

Serve this sauce with duck or lamb roast, or use it as a glaze in the last 15 to 20 min of cooking your roast.

3 tbsp. (45 mL) granulated sugar
6 tbsp. (90 mL) apple cider vinegar
1/2 cup (125 mL) chicken stock
1/2 cup (125 mL) chopped hyssop
  leaves
2 tsp. (10 mL) cornstarch
2 tbsp. (30 mL) water

Combine sugar, vinegar and chicken stock in a medium pot and bring to a boil. Add hyssop leaves and reduce heat to low. Simmer for about 30 minutes. Combine cornstarch and water in a bowl, whisk into a froth and add to sauce. Bring to a boil and cook until thickened. Store in refrigerator for up to 1 week. Makes 1 cup (250 mL).

Glazed Carrots with Hyssop

2 large carrots, thinly sliced
1 cup (250 mL) chicken stock
1 tbsp. (15 mL) honey
1 tbsp. (15 mL) butter
Salt, to taste
Freshly ground white pepper, to taste
1 tbsp. (15 mL) finely chopped fresh
  hyssop leaves

In a saucepan, combine carrots, chicken stock, honey, butter, salt and pepper. Bring to a simmer over medium heat. Cover, reduce heat to low and cook until carrots are tender and liquid is a syrupy glaze, about 20 minutes. Toss carrots with hyssop and serve immediately. Makes 4 servings.

Meatballs with Hyssop

1 1/2 cups (375 mL) ground pork
  or beef
1 medium onion, minced
2 tbsp. (30 mL) finely chopped
  fresh parsley
1 tbsp. (15 mL) finely chopped
  fresh hyssop
Salt, to taste
Pepper, to taste
1 large egg, fork-beaten
1/4 cup (60 mL) seasoned flour
3 tbsp. (45 mL) cooking oil

Combine meat, onion, parsley, hyssop, salt and pepper in a large bowl. Stir in beaten egg and mix well. Form into small balls and roll in seasoned flour. Heat oil in a large frying pan over high. Add meatballs and cook for 20 to 30 minutes, until they are brown, turning to brown on all sides. Reduce heat and cook a little longer if they are not cooked in centre. Makes 4 servings.

Wild Mint

Mentha arvensis

A perennial herb, growing 15 to 50 cm (6 to 20") in height, mint prefers moist, fertile soils and is often found in riparian areas. The plant has serrated leaves that culminate in an oval-shaped tip, with blue or pink flower spikes. All members of the mint family share an interesting characteristic—a unique square-shaped stem.

Food
Mint is widely used in teas, seasonings and candy flavourings.

Medicine
Mint is good for digestion, so chewing a mint leaf after you eat will do more then just freshen your breath. Mint is also used in ointments to help soothe sore muscles. Mint tea is used for coughs, colds and sore throats.

Cucumber, Mint and Yogurt Salad

Cucumber, Mint and Yogurt Salad

1 medium cucumber
1 small onion
2 garlic cloves
1 tbsp. (15 mL) chopped parsley leaves
1 tbsp. (15 mL) chopped mint leaves
2 cups (500 mL) natural yogurt
1/4 tsp. (1 mL) paprika
Mint leaves, for garnish

Finely chop cucumber, onion and garlic. Chop herbs and add to cucumber mixture. Stir in yogurt and paprika. Garnish with mint leaves. Serve chilled. Makes 5 servings.

Mint Sorbet

1 cup (250 mL) fresh mint leaves
3 cups (750 mL) water
3/4 cup (175 mL) granulated sugar
Juice of 1/2 fresh lime

Add mint leaves and water to a medium pot and bring to a boil. Reduce heat and simmer for 5 minutes. Remove from heat. Add sugar and stir until dissolved. Return to heat and simmer, covered, for 5 minutes. Set aside to cool. Add lime juice and puree with a blender. Strain juice into a freezer-safe container and place in freezer, or transfer mixture to an ice cream maker. Stir after 2 hours if you are not using an ice cream maker. Mixture should be slushy. Garnish with a mint leaf and serve. Makes 4 servings.

Mint and Rosemary Jelly

To make your jelly into a marinade, add 1/4 cup (60 mL) of red or white wine (depending on your meat choice), 2 tbsp. (30 mL) of lemon juice and 1 tbsp. (15 mL) of cooking oil. Mash together and marinade meat or vegetables of your choice; you can do this with most of the jelly recipes in this book.

7 cups (1.75 mL) apple juice
1/4 cup (60 mL) chopped fresh rosemary
1/2 cup (125 mL) chopped fresh mint leaves
1 tbsp. (15 mL) dried crushed chilies
7 1/2 cups (1.9 L) granulated sugar
1 (2 oz., 57 g) package of pectin

Heat apple juice in a large pot over medium-high and bring to a boil. Add remaining ingredients, bring to a slow boil and cook until mixture thickens. Sterilize jars and lids. Pour jelly into jars and let set. Makes 6 cups (1.5 L).

Mint Pesto

1 cup (250 mL) mint leaves
1/3 cup (75 mL) roasted, salted and shelled pistachios
1 small garlic clove, peeled
1/4 tsp. (1 mL) salt
1/4 cup (60 mL) extra virgin olive oil
1/4 tsp. (1 mL) lime juice

Combine mint leaves, pistachios, garlic and salt in a small food processor. Process until coarsely ground. In a steady stream, add oil and lime juice until mixture forms a paste. Store in refrigerator for up to 2 weeks. Makes 2 cups (500 mL).

Pearl Couscous with Mint and Pecans

2 tbsp. (30 mL) olive oil
1 medium-sized red onion, cut into slivers
1/4 cup (60 mL) pecans, chopped
1/2 cup (125 mL) pearl couscous
2/3 cup (150 mL) boiling water
1/4 cup (60 mL) fresh mint, chopped
1 tbsp. (15 mL) red wine vinegar
1 tbsp. (15 mL) olive oil
Salt, to taste
Pepper, to taste
Whole mint leaves, for garnish

Heat first amount of oil in a large frying pan over medium. Add onions and cook, stirring occasionally, until soft and slightly caramelized, about 20 minutes. Toast pecans in a small frying pan over low heat, stirring often, until golden and aromatic, about 5 minutes. Place couscous in a medium-large bowl and pour boiling water over top. Let stand, covered, for about 12 minutes. Remove lid and add onions, pecans, chopped mint, vinegar and remaining olive oil. Season with salt and pepper. Stir until evenly mixed. Garnish with whole mint leaves. Makes 5 servings.

Panzanella with Anchovy and Mint

I like to use my hands to toss panzanella to ensure the juices penetrate the bread.

1 lb. (454 g) cherry tomatoes
1 tsp. (5 mL) kosher or sea salt
5 oz. (140 g) day-old peasant bread, torn into bite-sized pieces
1 cucumber, peeled, seeds removed and chopped
1/2 small red onion, thinly sliced
2 tbsp. (30 mL) drained capers
2 tbsp. (30 mL) fresh mint, sliced into thin ribbons
2 anchovy fillets
1 garlic clove
1 tbsp. (15 mL) fresh mint, sliced into thin ribbons
Salt, to taste
Pepper, to taste
1/3 cup (75 mL) olive oil
2 tbsp. (30 mL) sherry vinegar
1 tbsp. (15 mL) fresh mint, sliced into thin ribbons

Slice tomatoes in halves or quarters and place in a colander over a bowl. Sprinkle tomatoes with salt and let stand for about 15 minutes. Reserve about 2 tbsp. (30 mL) of juice from bowl and place drained tomatoes in a large salad bowl with bread chunks, cucumber, onion, capers and first amount of sliced mint.

For the dressing, combine anchovies, garlic, second amount of mint, salt and pepper in a mortar and pestle or food processor until it forms a paste.

Add olive oil and vinegar to reserved tomato juice. Drop in anchovy paste and whisk until emulsified. Alternatively, mixture can be shaken in a jar. Adjust seasoning, if necessary. Pour dressing over salad and gently toss. Allow salad to stand at room temperature for at least 1 hour before serving. Garnish with remaining fresh mint. Makes 5 servings.

Shepherd's Purse

Capsella bursa-pastoris

A member of the mustard family, shepherd's purse is a weedy annual plant found along roadsides and in disturbed grounds. The plant develops from a rosette of lobed leaves at the base. Its stem grows to approximately 20 to 50 cm (8 to 20") in height and bears a few pointed leaves that partially grasp the stem. Shepherd's purse bears loose, small, white flowers and produces a heart-shaped seedpod.

Food

Shepherd's purse is a familiar ingredient in Asian markets. Commonly used in Shanghai, this plant can be found stir-fried with rice cakes, or mixed with other ingredients

for wonton fillings. In Korea it is known as *naengi,* and the roots are among several ingredients found in Korean soups and salads. Shepherd's purse cooks like a green vegetable, and the young leaves and seedpods have a peppery flavour that is very tasty in salads. Seeds from the plant are sometimes found in commercial bird feed. Shepherd's purse is high in vitamin C.

Medicine

Tea made from this plant was used to treat headaches and stomach issues.

Long Soup

Long Soup

6 cups (1.5 L) chicken stock
1 carrot, shredded
2 tbsp. (30 mL) shepherd's purse seeds
3/4 cup (175 mL) Chinese cabbage, shredded
1/2 cup (125 mL) rice noodles
1 cup (250 mL) thin strips of pork
1 1/2 tbsp. (22 mL) sesame oil
1/2 tsp. (2 mL) minced ginger root
2 tbsp. (30 mL) soy sauce
8 green onions, julienned

Bring chicken stock to a boil. Add shredded carrots, shepherd's purse seeds and cabbage and bring to a boil. Add rice noodles and cook for 7 minutes. Add pork and remaining ingredients. Cook for 3 to 4 minutes, until meat is no longer pink, being careful not to over cook. Makes 5 servings.

Mature stinging nettle with seed – the plant's tiny hairs will cause irritation at this stage.

Stinging Nettle

Urtica dioica

Nettle is a weedy perennial herb that grows to 2 m (7')
in height. It is found growing in moist, fertile soils.
Nettle flowers form pinkish spikes with pointed,
oval leaves that are toothed on the edges. As nettle
matures, it becomes very fibrous and is a known
skin irritant.

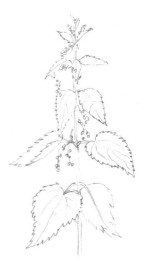

Food

Young growth is edible, but do not eat the mature
growth. Wear gloves to remove the leaves or young
tops from the stems. Use the early, young and tender
sprigs in salads or cook the nettle like spinach or for
cream of nettle soup. Nettle is high in vitamins A and
C and certain beneficial minerals.

Medicine

Today, nettle extracts are used in commercial lineament for sore muscles.

Other Uses

The stem of mature plants can be made into rope in the fall as the plant dries and the hairs fall off. During the Middle Ages, nettle products included clothing, paper, rope and fishnets. Historically, Roman soldiers were said to rub nettles on their skin for warmth and to prevent themselves from sleeping while on duty.

Nettle Soup

Serve this soup topped with roasted almonds, crispy bacon or croutons.

3 tbsp. (45 mL) butter

1 medium onion, chopped

1 garlic clove, minced

1/2 tsp. (2 mL) sugar

2 cups (500 mL) chopped, young nettle leaves

1 1/2 cups (375 mL) chicken stock

1/2 cup (125 mL) cream

1/4 tsp. (1 mL) ground nutmeg

Salt, to taste

Pepper, to taste

Melt butter in a medium saucepan over medium heat. Add onions and cook until caramelized, about 20 minutes. Add garlic, sugar and nettle leaves and cook until leaves are tender. Add chicken stock and bring to a boil. Cook for 2 to 3 minutes. Reduce heat and add cream, nutmeg, salt and pepper. Simmer for 3 to 4 minutes. Makes 5 servings.

Nettle Puree

Serve this dish as a vegetable side. For a variation, combine the mixture with cooked oatmeal, roll into balls and fry in bacon fat.

2 cups (500 mL) nettle leaves

2 tbsp. (30 mL) butter

1 medium onion, chopped

Salt, to taste

Pepper, to taste

To help remove hairs, cook leaves in a steamer for about 4 minutes, then rinse leaves under tap water in a strainer. Strain any excess water. Melt butter in a medium saucepan over medium. Add onion and cook until tender. Mash in leaves and season with salt and pepper. Reduce heat and simmer for 5 minutes. Makes 5 servings.

Risotto with Nettles

Wear gloves to remove the young nettle leaves from the stems.

2 cups (500 mL) homemade chicken stock

2 cups (500 mL) water

2 tbsp. (30 mL) extra virgin olive oil

1 small yellow onion, minced

1 cup (250 mL) risotto rice

6 oz. (170 g) nettle leaves, stems removed

3/4 cup (175 mL) dry white wine

Salt, to taste

Pepper, to taste

1 tbsp. (15 mL) unsalted butter

3/4 cup (175 mL) finely grated Parmigiano Reggiano

Combine chicken stock and water in a saucepan and heat until hot but not boiling. Reduce heat to low and maintain heat just below a simmer.

Heat olive oil in a large heavy casserole dish over medium. Add onions and cook, stirring occasionally, until soft. Add rice and nettles. Stir for 2 to 3 minutes to toast rice and coat with oil. Add wine and simmer, stirring constantly, until wine is reduced by half, about 3 to 4 minutes. Add a ladleful of stock to rice, stirring in rice from sides and bottom of pot. Continue to stir until most of liquid has been absorbed. Add another ladleful of stock and continue to stir until liquid has been almost absorbed. Continue to add stock and stir in the same manner until rice is no longer chalky, about 20 to 25 minutes in total. Season with salt and pepper. Remove from heat and add another ladleful of stock, as well as butter and half of cheese. Return to heat until cheese and butter are melted. Cover pan and remove from heat. Let stand for 5 minutes. Remove cover and stir. Serve immediately with remaining cheese on top. Makes 5 servings.

Nettle Frittata

1/2 cup (125 mL) cleaned young nettle tops
3 tbsp. (45 mL) extra virgin olive oil
1 garlic clove, minced
6 large eggs
Salt, to taste
Pepper, to taste
1/4 cup (60 mL) heavy cream
1 tbsp. (15 mL) extra virgin olive oil

Heat 1/3 of nettles and 1 tbsp. (15 mL) olive oil in a non-stick pan over medium. Cook until tender, adding a small amount of water if needed. Remove nettles from pan and set aside. Repeat with remaining nettles, adding garlic to third batch. Place cooked nettles on a cutting board and chop finely. Transfer to a food

processor and add eggs, salt and pepper. Mix until nettles are fully incorporated into eggs. Add cream and mix for 10 seconds.

Heat remaining oil in an oven-proof non-stick pan over medium. Add nettle mixture and stir with a rubber spatula to get entire mixture warm. Cook in 300°F (150°C) oven for about 12 minutes, until set in center. Let stand for 3 minutes to cool. Turn out onto a plate and serve. Makes 5 servings.

Nettle, Mint and Melon Iced Tea

Cut some honeydew melon into 1 inch (2.5 cm) cubes, freeze them and use them as ice cubes in this iced tea.

4 2/3 cups (1.15 L) water
1 1/2 cups (375 mL) honeydew melon, peeled and chopped
1/4 cup (60 mL) fresh mint leaves, tightly packed
1/4 cup (60 mL) stinging nettle

In a saucepot bring water and melon to a boil. Add mint and nettle, and simmer for 5 minutes. Set aside to steep for 2 minutes, then pour through a strainer into a juice container and refrigerate. Makes 6 servings.

Breadroot in early flower

Indian Breadroot

Psoralea esculenta

Also called: wild turnip

This perennial is often found in open, native prairie on well-drained, rocky or sandy soils. The plant has a broad range and is native to the prairies of the Great Plains and northwest regions of North America. This species is adapted to disturbed soil and was plentiful when the bison roamed the plains. In spring, stems form from the ground and reach up to 30 cm (1') in height. The leaves are palmately divided into 5 leaflets.

Both the stem and leaves are extremely hairy. In early summer the plant produces several blue or purple blooms in clusters about 2 to 10 cm (3/4 to 4") long, made up of numerous florets forming a cone shape. It is best harvested from May through July when the blooming flower stalks make it easier to find. When it finishes flowering and goes to seed, the aerial parts dry up and the stalks break off, disappearing quickly. Breadroot was once found growing abundantly; however, much of its prairie habitat has been converted to farmland or managed grassland. I have limited experience with this plant; though it is not considered rare, breadroot seems to be getting harder to find. I have finally managed to get several of these plants to grow in a sandy area of my yard, so I hope to be cooking with it soon.

Food

The tuberous root of breadroot was an important food source for Indigenous people of the plains. It has a potato-like consistency and is edible cooked or raw. Traditional preparation included drying and grinding the root into powder or meal for porridge. Breadroot can also be eaten raw in salads and cooked in soups and stews.

128

Medicine

The starch in breadroot may be beneficial for people with diabetes as the starch does not convert to sugar during digestion.

Roasted Breadroot with Onions and Carrots

The breadroot needs to soak for a few days before this recipe can be prepared, so plan accordingly.

4 breadroot tubers

2 small onions

2 medium carrots, chopped in 1" (2.5 cm) pieces

Salt, to taste

Pepper, to taste

1 1/2 tsp. (7 mL) dill seed

1 1/2 tsp. (7 mL) cumin seed

2 tbsp (30 mL) cooking oil

Soak breadroot in water for 2 or 3 days in the refrigerator. The soaking water does not need to be changed. Bring a large pot of water to a boil over medium and add breadroot. Cook for 20 minutes. Remove from water and set aside to cool. Peel cooled breadroot and cut into pieces about 1" (2.5 cm) long. Quarter onions and separate them into 2 or 3 layers. Place breadroot, onions and carrots into a mixing bowl and stir in remaining 5 ingredients. Transfer to a baking sheet and cook in 375°F (190°C) oven for 30 to 40 minutes, until golden brown and tender. Makes 4 servings.

Breadroot Porridge

Breadroot porridge was one of the most common uses of the plant by Indigenous peoples. The following recipe borrows elements from a recipe found in Snell (2006) as well as some incorporation of personal experience.

To make breadroot meal, soak the roots for 2 or 3 days, then dry them on a rack in the sun. Placing black paper under the rack will speed up the process. Once the breadroots have dried, use a food processor to grind them to a cornmeal consistency.

2 cups (500 mL) of ground breadroot meal

2 2/3 cups (650 mL) warm water

3 tbsp. (45 mL) wheat flour

2 tbsp. (30 mL) marrowfat

1/2 cup (125 mL) saskatoon berries

1/4 cup (60 mL) toasted shelled sunflower seeds

Salt, to taste

Granulated sugar, to taste

Place breadroot meal in warm water in a saucepan until meal softens. Simmer over medium until tender, about 30 minutes. Mix wheat flour with just enough water to make a paste and add to breadroot mixture, stirring energetically until mixture is smooth with no lumps. Bring to a boil and cook, covered, for 5 minutes. Stir in marrowfat, saskatoon berries and sunflower seeds, and remove from heat. Add salt and sugar to taste. Makes 6 servings.

Wild Licorice

Glycyrrhiza lepidota

This weedy-looking plant is generally found in moist to dry sandy soils in grasslands and riparian areas, growing to a height of 30 cm to 1 m (1 to 3'). Licorice is a perennial with a white or sometimes yellowish flower. The flower heads have several blooms that form a cone shape, and the individual flowers are similar to dragon snaps. During fall, these blossoms ripen into burs, the spines of which cover the oval-shaped seedpods.

Food

Wild licorice roots have been used for medicinal and nutritional purposes by plains Indigenous peoples; however, there is contemporary debate about the potential side effects of the plants. The European species, *G. glabra*, is cultivated. As a root crop, the young tender roots are sweet and edible when raw. European licorice is large, and extracts are used as a commercial flavouring in candies and throat lozenges.

Medicine

Licorice has been used to reduce fevers and settle upset stomachs or as a tea for sore throats.

Other Uses

In earlier societies the rootstocks were used as toothbrushes and are sometimes still used this way today.

Pork Tenderloin with Wild Licorice Sauce, stuffed tomato, aromatic rice and flatbread

Pork Tenderloin with Wild Licorice Sauce

5 licorice root sticks, about
   4" (10 cm) long, peeled
2 cups (500 mL) chicken stock
1/2 tbsp. (7 mL) cumin seeds
1/4 tsp. (1 mL) crushed fennel seeds
1 tsp. (5 mL) orange juice
Grated zest from 1 lime
Pork tenderloin roast (about 2 lbs.,
   900 g)
2 tbsp. (30 mL) butter
2 tbsp. (30 mL) flour
1 tbsp. (15 mL) garden cress
Pistachios, for garnish

Set 1 licorice root aside. Make licorice extract by boiling other 4 licorice root sticks in stock until the liquid is reduced to about 1 cup (250 mL).

Toast cumin and fennel in a frying pan over medium until fragrant, about 30 seconds. Transfer to a mortar and grind spices and remaining licorice stick into powder using a pestle. Combine spices, orange juice, lime zest and licorice extract in a medium saucepan. Place roast in a large bowl with a lid and pour mixture over top. Marinate, covered and refrigerated, for at least 2 hours, or overnight.

Remove pork from bowl and return marinade to fridge. In a large frying pan over medium, sear pork on all sides. Transfer to a meat loaf pan and cook in 350°F (175°C) oven for about three quarters of its normal cooking time—time will vary, depending on size of roast. Add reserved marinade and cook, covered, for about 30 minutes. Remove pork from pan and set aside, wrapped in aluminum foil.

Transfer marinade to a frying pan and heat over medium-high. Cook until reduced to about 1 cup (250 mL). Combine butter and flour in a small bowl to make a roux. Still into marinade to thicken. Slice meat and drizzle with sauce. Sprinkle with cress and a bit of lime zest. Top with toasted pistachios. Makes 5 servings.

Venison with Licorice Root, Juniper and Saskatoon Berry Sauce

2 lbs. (900 g) venison loin
1/4 cup (60 mL) corn oil
2 tbsp. (30 mL) juniper berries, crushed
2 tbsp. (30 mL) corn oil
1 small tomato, chopped
2 peeled licorice roots
1/4 cup (60 mL) coarsely chopped
   onion
2 tbsp. (30 mL) chopped carrot
1/2 cup (125 mL) red wine
1 tsp. (5 mL) honey
1 tbsp. (15 mL) apple cider vinegar
1/2 cup (125 mL) saskatoon berries
2 cups (500 mL) beef stock
Salt, to taste
Pepper, to taste

Cut venison into 6 pieces and pour first amount of oil over top. Sprinkle with juniper berries, and marinate in the refrigerator for at least 4 hours or overnight.

For the sauce, heat remaining oil, tomato, licorice root, onion and carrot in a heavy bottomed saucepan over a medium-high. Cook for about 10 minutes, stirring frequently, until vegetables are golden brown. Add wine, bring to a boil and reduce heat to a simmer. Add honey, vinegar and berries, and cook for about 10 minutes, stirring occasionally and crushing berries with back of a spoon. Add beef stock. Strain mixture and discard solids. Simmer sauce until it is reduced and thickened to a consistency similar to heavy cream.

Season venison with salt and pepper. Grill on direct heat to get a sear on all sides, about 1 to 2 minutes per side (ideally, over hot hardwood coals) and then place over indirect heat and cook, covered, for about 7 to 12 minutes per side. Remove from heat and let stand for a few minutes. To serve, spoon sauce over meat and serve remaining sauce on side. Makes 5 servings.

I was once working during an overnight outing with a group of children and I pulled a piece of wild licorice root out of my pack. Immediately, a young Middle Eastern boy pulled a piece of licorice root from his pocket. He told me, with a blinding smile, that he had bought his root at a grocery store specializing in Middle Eastern foods. He used it as a toothbrush during the entire trip, and I must say that he had beautiful teeth.

Strawberry flower

Strawberry fruit

Wild Strawberry

Fragaria spp.

At least 2 species of wild strawberry are found on the Prairies, including the field strawberry *(F. virginiana)* and the woodland strawberry *(F. vesca)*. These perennial plants prefer growing in moist, wooded areas, in grasslands or pastures and are often found in prairie roadside ditches. All strawberries, including wild species and cultivated varieties, develop from a fibrous root with short, creeping rhizomes and have a low-growing, creeping growth habit reaching 5 to 10 cm (2 to 4") high. They have long, slender, leafless red runners (called stolons) that form into new plants when they come into contact with the soil. The oval-shaped leaflets are approximately 2 to 7 cm (3/4 to 2 3/4") long and are divided into 3 sides, with toothed edges. Strawberry flowers are small with 5 white petals and yellow centres. The fruit of the wild strawberry is small but full of flavour. Both wild and cultivated strawberries can be used interchangeably in cooking. Strawberry seeds are tiny pips or achenes embedded in the outside surface of the fruit.

Food
The fruit of the wild strawberry is high in vitamin C and is good in jams and pies. It is also delicious eaten raw.

Medicine
Tea from the leaves was traditionally used to reduce fevers. Cold tea was used as a wash for skin issues like eczema.

Strawberry Jam

To add a twist to your jam, add 1 tsp. (5 mL) of anise seed while the jam is boiling and let the flavours blend.

6 1/2 cups (1.6 L) crushed or sliced strawberries
4 cups (1 L) granulated sugar
1 (2 oz., 57 g) package of pectin

Combine strawberries, sugar and pectin in a large pot and bring to a boil. Reduce heat and simmer until mixture thickens. Pour into sterilized jars. Makes 6 cups (1.5 L).

Strawberry Vinegar

4 cups (1 L) strawberries
1 cup (250 mL) red wine vinegar
3/4 cup (175 mL) granulated sugar

Soak strawberries in vinegar for 4 days. Combine strawberry mixture with sugar in a large pot and bring to a boil. Remove from heat as soon as mixture reaches a boil. Set aside to cool. Strain and pour into sterilized jars. Makes 5 cups (1.25 L).

Strawberry Salad

Add a poached chicken breast, cooled and sliced, to create a whole meal.

1/3 cup (75 mL) strawberry vinegar (see above)
1/2 cup (125 mL) granulated sugar
1 tsp. (5 mL) dry mustard
3/4 cup (175 mL) vegetable oil
2 tsp. (10 mL) poppy seeds
1/2 cup (125 mL) sliced almonds or pecans
1 lb. (454 g) spinach, larger stems removed
1 cup (250 mL) sliced strawberries

Combine first 5 ingredients in a spill-proof bottle and shake well. Set aside.

Toast nuts in a frying pan over medium heat. Set aside to cool. Toss nuts with spinach and strawberries in a serving bowl. Drizzle with dressing and serve. Makes 5 servings.

Strawberry Pie

For a different flavour, I like to add about 1/2 cup (125 mL) rhubarb stem (rhubarb leaves are poisonous) and some additional sugar to the boiling fruit punch mixture. Another way to add a twist is to add 1/2 tsp. (2 mL) of anise seed or 1 tbsp. (15 mL) of hyssop leaves to the mixture while it is boiling.

1 (9", 23 cm) pie shell
1 (3 oz., 85 g) box of strawberry jelly powder (gelatine)
2 tbsp. (30 mL) cornstarch
1/2 cup (125 mL) granulated sugar
1 1/2 cups (375 mL) fruit punch
1 1/2 cups (375 mL) strawberries
Whipped cream, for garnish

Bake pie shell in 375°F (190°C) oven for 7 to 10 minutes. Set aide to cool.

In a medium saucepan, combine jelly powder and cornstarch. Stir in sugar and fruit punch. Cook over medium heat until mixture boils, stirring slowly. Remove from heat and set aside to cool slightly. Slice strawberries into pie shell. Pour warm fruit punch mixture over strawberries (mixture should be warm enough to soften strawberries). Let pie cool before placing it in refrigerator so crust does not get soggy. Transfer to refrigerator and let stand until set. Serve individual slices with a dollop of whipped cream. Cuts into 8 wedges.

White wood violet

Early blue violet

Violets

Viola spp.

Many violet species grow across Canada and the Prairies. Habitat is dependent on the species and may include dry open prairie grassland, meadows, open woods, thickets, bogs and riparian zones. Violets are low-growing perennial plants that grow up to 15 cm (6 ") in height. Typically, the leaves are egg- to heart- to kidney-shaped. The flowers grow in a variety of colours, including blue, pink, purple and white, and have 5 (often unequal) petals, usually with 2 on the top and 3 at the bottom.

Food

The flowers and leaves of all violets are edible, including the common introduced varieties such as johnny jump ups. The flowers and leaves are high in vitamin A and C and are good in salads and as a garnish. White wood violet flowers (*V. canadensis*) have an edible central thread in the leaves that has a wintergreen taste. However, the rhizomes, fruits and/or seeds of some violets are **poisonous**. Further, several species of native violets are rare. Consult a local flora and check government conservation websites, and harvest with care.

Medicine

All violets including the garden varieties contain salicylic acid, which is known to reduce swelling and fever. Tea made from violets has been used to treat bronchitis, asthma, coughs and sore throats. Cool tea was used to treat skin issues such as eczema.

Wildflower Salad

1/2 cup (125 mL) walnuts
1/3 cup (75 mL) violet blossoms
2 cups (500 mL) violet leaves
1 cup (250 mL) young dandelion greens
1/4 cup (60 mL) iceberg lettuce
4 cups (1 L) lettuce
1/2 cup (125 mL) mandarin oranges,
  drained
1/2 cup (125 mL) fresh or partially
  thawed frozen raspberries
Raspberry or tangerine vinaigrette,
  to serve

Toast walnuts and set aside to cool.
Toss all ingredients together, and serve
with fruit vinaigrette. Makes 5 servings.

Violet and Radish Spring Salad with Lemon-Garlic Dressing

*The dressing is best if you add a drizzle of
leftover pan-drippings, preferably chicken.
You can substitute sunflower oil for the
olive oil, if desired.*

1/2 cup (125 mL) violet flowers
  and leaves, stems removed
1 1/2 lbs. (680 g) mixed lettuce leaves
2 tsp. (10 mL) lemon juice
2 tsp. (10 mL) olive oil
1 garlic clove, crushed
Salt, to taste
Pepper, to taste
8 radishes, sliced

Rinse and dry all your greens and flowers, and place them in a large bowl.

Combine lemon juice, oil and garlic in
a jar with a lid and shake until well combined. Add salt and pepper to taste.
Pour over greens, add radishes and toss
until greens are coated. Sprinkle flowers
over top. Makes 4 servings.

Oranges and Violet

1 orange
1/2 tsp. (2 mL) honey
Orange liquor, to taste (optional)
20 violet flowers

Remove orange peel, leaving as little pith
as possible. Cut flesh into 1/3" (1 cm)
slices, drizzle with honey, sprinkle with
orange liquor, if using, and garnish with
fresh violets. Makes 4 servings.

Violet Jelly

2 cups (500 mL) fresh violet blossoms
2 cups (500 mL) boiling water
Juice from 1 lemon
1 (2 oz., 57 g) package of pectin
4 cups (1 L) granulated sugar

Place violet blossoms in a glass jar and
cover with boiling water. Let stand, covered, for 24 hours. The water will change
to aqua blue. Strain liquid into a glass
bowl and press out all water from flowers. Discard flowers. Add lemon juice.
The mixture will change to a pink hue.
Pour mixture into a stockpot and stir in
pectin. Bring to a boil. Add sugar and
boil vigorously for 1 minute. Remove and
discard any foam that forms on surface.
Pour mixture into sterile jars and seal.
Makes approximately 2 1/2 cups
(625 mL).

Violet Syrup

4 cups (1 L) violet blossoms
2 cups (500 mL) boiling water
6 cups (1.5 L) granulated sugar
Juice from 1 lemon
2 cups (500 mL) fruit punch

Place violets in a glass jar and pour boiling water over top. Let stand, covered,
for 24 hours. Strain liquid into a glass
bowl and press out all water from

flowers. Discard flowers. Combine sugar, lemon juice and fruit punch in a saucepan. Bring to a boil and cook until mixture thickens into syrup. Add violet water and boil for 10 minutes or until thickened. Pour into sterilized bottles. Set aside to cool. Store in refrigerator for up to 1 month. Makes about 6 cups (1.5 L)

Candied Violets

Use these violets as a garnish or store them in the fridge in a sealed container if you won't be using them right away.

1 large egg white
20 violet flowers, with about 2" (5 cm) of stem attached
2 tbsp. (30 mL) icing (or confectioner's) sugar

Beat egg white until frothy but not too stiff. Holding stem, dip violet flower into egg white, twirling gently to coat entire flower. Shake off excess egg white. Using a sifter, shake powdered sugar over flower. Twirl flower stem, holding it so flower gets evenly coated with sugar on all sides. Place on a clean tea towel on a cookie sheet. Repeat with remaining flowers, spacing them on sheet so they do not touch each other. Refrigerate, uncovered, for 24 hours. As flowers dry, most of sugar will be absorbed by egg white, creating a glaze on petals.

Remove cookie sheet from refrigerator and let flowers stand at room temperature in a warm part of your home for 24 hours. Snip off and discard stems. Makes 20 candied violets.

Violet Cupcakes with Cream Cheese Frosting

Garnish these cupcakes with candied violets (see this page) for an extra special presentation.

8 oz. (225 g) cream cheese, softened
1/2 cup (125 mL) butter, softened
3/4 cup (175 mL) granulated sugar
2 eggs
2 cups (500 mL) flour
2 tsp. (10 mL) baking powder
1/2 tsp. (2 L) salt
1 cup (250 mL) milk
1 tsp. (5 mL) vanilla extract
1 tbsp. (15 mL) ground dried violet flowers
1/2 cup (125 mL) cup unsalted butter, softened
1 1/3 cups (325 mL) sifted confectioners' sugar
1 tsp. (5 mL) vanilla extract

Remove cream cheese from fridge and set aside to warm to room temperature. Cream together first amount of butter and sugar until light and fluffy. In a separate bowl, beat eggs, and then slowly add to butter mixture.

Combine next 3 ingredients in a medium bowl. Slowly add to butter mixture. Add milk and beat well. Stir in vanilla and ground violet. Divide batter evenly into muffin pans lined with paper cupcake liners. Bake in 375°F (190°C) for about 18 minutes. Allow to cool in pans before removing.

For the icing beat together cream cheese and remaining butter with an electric mixer. Gradually add confectioners' sugar, beating until icing has a smooth, creamy consistency. Add remaining vanilla extract and beat until well combined. Smooth over cooled cupcakes with a spatula.

Wetland Plants

Thus far, the focus has been on terrestrial sources of wild food. Aquatic and semi-aquatic plants also offer a wide variety of food possibilities. Take care if harvesting plants from wet areas, as wetlands are sensitive habitats. Further, as many of these plants act as filters, avoid polluted or contaminated waters as the plants may accumulate toxins.

Arrowhead

Sagittaria latifolia

The plant is circumpolar and grows in shallow standing to slow-moving water, to a height of 20 to 50 cm (8 to 20"). It has a perennial rhizome that is a horizontal creeper. Arrowhead leaves are projectile point in shape. The flower is white and has 3 petals. The fruit is contained within a spiked pod.

Food

High in starch and similar in taste to water chestnuts, arrowhead tubers were a highly valued, versatile food source for Indigenous North Americans. Arrowhead plants were consumed raw, dried, boiled, baked, roasted and mashed, as well as being ground into flour or candied with maple sugar. Though the skin is edible, arrowhead tubers are more palatable when peeled. The Cheyenne gathered the plant stalks below the flowers, peeled them and ate them raw. These tubers are also a favourite food of beavers and muskrats. The best time to collect tubers is in the fall or early spring. One method of harvesting is to wiggle your toes in the mud to release the tubers, which then float to the surface. Remove the tuber growing at the end of each rhizome, scrub the tubers clean and boil them in salted water for 15 minutes.

Medicine

Traditionally, tea made from the root of the plant has been used to treat symptoms of heartburn. The leaves were eaten to relieve headaches.

Roasted Arrowhead Tubers

If you want to add a little extra flavour to this dish, add dill, caraway or cumin seeds.

1 cup (250 mL) arrowhead tubers
2 shallots, chopped
1 garlic clove, chopped
Salt, to taste
Pepper, to taste
2 tbsp. (30 mL) cooking oil

Place first 5 ingredients into a large bowl. Drizzle oil over top and stir until tubers, shallots and garlic are evenly coated with oil. Transfer to a cookie sheet and roast in 350°F (175°C) oven for 20 to 30 minutes, until golden brown. Makes 4 servings.

Chinese Arrowhead

10 arrowhead tubers
1/4 cup (60 mL) coarse salt
2 tbsp. (30 mL) sesame oil
1 garlic clove, minced
1 tsp. (5 mL) dried crushed chilies
4 scallions, chopped
1 tbsp. (15 mL) roasted sesame seeds
1 tbsp. (15 mL) fish sauce or oyster
　sauce

Wash arrowhead tubers in warm water. Spread coarse salt in a layer on a baking tray or a loaf pan. Place tubers on top of salt and cover with aluminum foil. Bake 350°F (175°C) oven for 75 minutes. Peel tubers while still warm and cut into quarters.

Heat sesame oil in a pan over medium-high. Stir-fry tubers until they reach a golden colour. Add garlic, chilies, scallions, sesame seeds and fish sauce. Toss and serve. Makes 4 servings.

Creamed Arrowhead Tubers

I often reserve the liquids from cooking starchy foods to water my houseplants and garden, after the liquid is cool, as a natural fertilizer.

2 cups (500 mL) arrowhead tubers,
　washed and scrubbed
1 tbsp. (15 mL) butter
1 small onion, chopped
2 celery stalks, chopped
2 carrots, chopped
1/4 cup (60 mL) sour cream
1/8 tsp. (0.5 mL) fresh thyme
Salt, to taste
Pepper, to taste

Slice arrowhead tubers and place into a large saucepan. Cover with water and boil gently until tender, about 20 to 30 minutes, then drain tubers.

Melt butter in a saucepan over medium heat. Add onion, celery and carrots and cook until tender. Combine vegetables, sour cream and seasonings with cooked tubers. Mix well and serve. Makes 5 servings.

Marsh marigold in flower

Marsh Marigold

Caltha palustris

Marsh marigold is a perennial found in single bunches approximately 20 to 60 cm (8" to 2') across in size. A member of the buttercup family, marsh marigold prefers wet soil with moving water. The plant boasts kidney-shaped leaves that may be slightly serrated or smooth on the margins. Flowers of the marsh marigold are usually yellow with carpels forming sac-like "fruit" containing numerous seeds.

Food

Older leaves, before the plant actually flowers, may be eaten if they are well cooked. The same is true for the flowers and roots. Marsh marigold roots must be boiled well. Flower buds may be cooked or pickled and used as a substitute for capers. Cook the young, spring leaves like spinach by bringing them to a boil, then changing the water and boiling again. Boil the roots for soup or stews. Given the risks associated with this plant, you should not use it unless you have conducted in-depth research.

WARNING: Once the plant starts to produce flowers it also produces toxins. Eating the raw leaves or flowers can lead to poisoning.

Medicine

Tea made from the leaves was used as a laxative.

Cattail cob

Cattail

Typha latifolia

This plant is found in marshy ground and wet areas, often on the edge of waterbodies. It grows up to 3 m (10') high with long, slender leaves, alternated and mainly basal on a simple, joint-less stem bearing flower spikes that form over a long, terminal spike. Cattail is monecious, meaning it has separate male and female flower parts on the same plant, which develop in dense racemes. The numerous male flowers of cattails form a narrow spike at the top of a vertical stem. During its growth cycle, each male flower divides into a pair of stamens and hairs that wither and expire after the release of pollen. Below the male counterpart, large numbers of tiny female flowers develop along a dense, elongated, oval-shaped spike, which resembles a cob. The seeds are extremely tiny and ripen into a light, cotton-like substance easily distributed over new growing areas by the wind.

Food

As cattails first start to grow, they can be plucked, stripped of their outer leaves and eaten raw in salads. The starchy tubers (young sub-surface stems similar to asparagus) and young flower spikes (cattail cobs) are delicious steamed and eaten with a little garlic butter. In early summer, the yellow pollen can be collected by tilting the top portion of the plant sideways, placing a paper bag over the end, then shaking the pollen from the cob. Once you have collected the pollen, sift it to remove all impurities such as spiders and stems. The sifted powder can then be added to flour and used for biscuits or cakes.

This plant is a smorgasbord of edible parts; however, it is a filtering plant and may retain toxins, waterborne bacteria and parasites, including giardia, commonly

known as "beaver fever." You need to
ensure that plants harvested are reliably
free of contamination and are not taken
from areas used for water treatment, near
industrial areas or fields routinely sprayed
with pesticides. Some towns in Saskatchewan use cattails to filter sewage; harmful
E. coli bacteria might be present if plants
are harvested from such an area. Plants
found growing in wet areas fed from
a spring are the best choice. I have two
small ponds in my yard, which provide
a fresh supply of cattails during the
summer.

Medicine
The slimy jelly in the stock of the plant was
used to treat wounds and burns.

Other Uses
Historically suitable to mobile or nomadic
lifestyles, mature cattail leaves were woven
into lightweight mats and baskets. Old-
world uses for cattails included using the leaves for thatching roofs and drying the
mature flowers for torches. Pioneers took the "fluff" from mature flowers to fill
mattresses and pillows; however, the flammable properties of the material contribute to the spread of house fires.

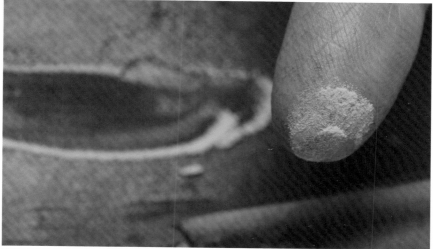

Yellowish cattail pollen, shaken from the flower spikes

Cattail Pollen Biscuits

Cattail Pollen Biscuits

Cattail pollen does not keep well, so it must be stored in the freezer if not used right away. Its short shelf life may be partly why this unique-tasting product is not commercially available.

1 cup (250 mL) cattail pollen
1 cup (250 mL) flour
1 tbsp. (15 mL) granulated sugar
1 1/2 tbsp. (22 mL) baking powder
1/3 cup (75 mL) butter, softened
3/4 cup (175 mL) milk

Combine dry ingredients in a large bowl. Add butter and blend into dry ingredients. Add milk and knead lightly. Form dough into 1 1/4" (3 cm) balls. Place on a cookie sheet and bake at 425°F (220°C) for 10 to 12 minutes. Makes 24 biscuits.

Roasted Cattail Tubers

To add extra flavour, toss in some dill, caraway or cumin seeds.

2 shallots, chopped
1 garlic clove, chopped
2 tbsp. (30 mL) cooking oil
Salt, to taste
Pepper, to taste
1 cup (250 mL) cattail tubers
1 tbsp. (15 mL) rosemary
1 tbsp. (15 mL) lemon juice

Combine all 8 ingredients in a medium bowl and stir to ensure oil coats ingredients evenly. Transfer to a baking sheet and roast at 350°F (175°C) for 20 to 30 minutes, until golden brown. Makes 4 servings.

Cat-on-the-Cob with Garlic Butter

Feel free to add the herbs of your choice to the garlic butter. The olive oil makes the butter creamy and easy to spread, even after refrigerating. I like to make a batch of this butter to keep handy in the fridge. You can also make a larger batch ahead of time to freeze in small containers so you are ready when the greens are in season.

25 young cattail flower heads (cobs)
1/2 cup (125 mL) unsalted butter
1/2 cup (125 mL) olive oil
Salt, to taste
12 garlic cloves, crushed
2 tbsp. (30 mL) chopped fresh chives
1 tbsp. (15 mL) fresh parsley

Peel any outer leaves from cattail flower heads. Boil flower heads in water for about 10 minutes. Drain and set aside.

For the garlic butter, whip butter, oil, salt, garlic, chives and parsley together in a food processor until smooth. Slather flower heads generously with garlic butter and eat them just like miniature corn on the cob. Makes 25 cobs.

Cattail Cob Stuffing

2 tbsp. (30 mL) butter
1 large onion, diced
1 tsp. (5 mL) fresh thyme
1 tsp. (5 mL) fresh sage
1 tsp. (5 mL) fresh rosemary
Salt, to taste
Pepper, to taste
1/4 cup (60 mL) raisins
1/4 cup (60 mL) dry cranberries
3/4 cup (175 mL) chicken stock
2 cups (500 mL) bread crumbs
2 1/2 (625 mL) cups of cattail cobs with centre stock removed
1/4 cup (60 mL) walnuts

Heat butter in a medium saucepan over medium. Add onion and cook until browned. Add herbs, raisins and cran-berries. Stir in chicken stock, bread crumbs and cattail cobs and mix well. Add walnuts just before serving to maintain their crunch.

Cattails with pollen

Salmon Soup with Arrowhead Tubers and Cattail Shoots

4 cups (1 L) chicken stock or vegetable stock
12 arrowhead tubers washed, peeled and cubed
6 cattail shoots, chopped
6 green onions or wild onions, chopped
5 juniper berries
1 lb. (454 g) salmon steak

In a deep saucepan or pot, combine stock, tubers, cattails, onions and juniper berries and bring to a boil. Reduce heat to medium and cook until arrowhead tubers are tender, about 15 minutes. Add salmon and cook for 8 to 10 minutes. Reduce heat to a simmer and remove salmon from pot. Debone and detach skin from salmon and discard. Break meat into smaller bite-size chunks and return to pot. Bring all ingredients to desired temperature and serve. Makes 4 servings.

Cattail Wild Rice Soup

1 cup (250 mL) dry wild rice
2 tbsp. (30 mL) sesame oil
1/2 cup (125 mL) chopped green onion
2 cups (500 mL) young cattail shoots, sliced
2 tsp. (10 mL) salt
4 cups (1 L) chicken stock

Cook wild rice according to package directions until tender. Heat oil in a heavy-bottomed pot over medium and cook onion and cattail shoots for about 10 minutes, until tender and shoots turn translucent. Stir in cooked wild rice, salt and chicken stock. Reduce heat and simmer for 15 to 20 minutes. Makes 5 servings.

Scouring Rush

Equisetum hyemale

Scouring rush is a perennial plant that grows in moist areas. Millions of years ago members of this genus grew as tall as pine trees. The contemporary scouring rush is characterized by a creeping rhizome and a single, hollow stem that is rough to the touch and grows to a height of 10 to 80 cm (4 to 32"). When I show this plant in my educational sessions, I demonstrate how to use the plant to file fingernails and joke with the girls that if you're lost in the woods and the helicopter is coming to rescue you, you might want to make sure your nails look good just in case the pilot is cute.

Medicine

This plant is good for cleansing minor wounds, reducing bleeding and mitigating infection.

Other Uses

Indigenous peoples have used the abrasive properties of the plant for polishing and cleaning. You can even file your nails or scrub pots with it.

147

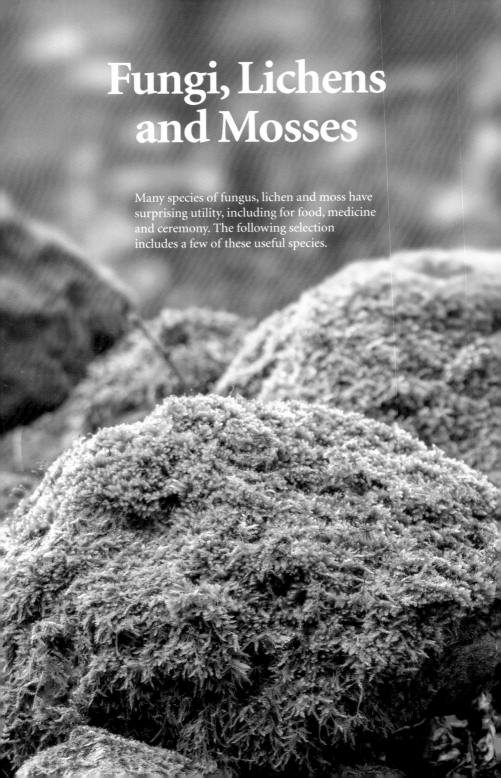

Fungi, Lichens and Mosses

Many species of fungus, lichen and moss have surprising utility, including for food, medicine and ceremony. The following selection includes a few of these useful species.

Hoof Fungus

Fomes fomentarius

This fungus grows exclusively on paper birch trees. It produces very large polypore fruiting bodies, similar in shape to a horse's hoof. The fruit is usually brown, though it can vary from shades of silver-grey to black. This fungus infects

Hoof fungus on a birch tree

through broken bark, causing rot, and continues to thrive on its host tree long after the host has died, altering its own living state from parasite to decomposer. Amadou is a substance created from the flesh of the fruit of a hoof fungus and can be used as combustible tinder for starting fires.

Medicine

Dentists used amadou for drying teeth, and surgeons used it as a styptic or anti-hemorrhagic.

Other Uses

This fungus has been used as early as 3000 BCE to create clothing, caps and gloves. It can also be used as a container to transport embers for strating fires. A contemporary discovery of a deceased and well preserved Ice-Age man, known as "The Iceman," found the individual

to be carrying pieces of amadou with him prior to his demise. To make a carrying device for embers, cut the fungus whole from its host tree and while still fresh, remove the gills, forming it into a bowl, which can then be used to hold or transfer the embers more safely from a fire. Extreme caution and common sense should be used if attempting to make and use such a device, given the obvious potential for fire and burn hazards.

Reindeer lichen

Lichen

Usnea spp. • *Byroria* spp. • *Cladonia* spp. and others

Lichen can be found growing on trees, rocks and sand. Lichens consist of two separate organisms: a fungus and an alga, existing in symbiosis. Lichens grow very slowly and have several different growth patterns and colours. Old man whisker *(Usnea* spp.)*, which often grows in the boreal forest, is usually a pale green. This flattened, stringy lichen has an almost leafy look and grows on trees and tall shrubs. Old man whisker is useful for starting fires and burns quickly. Other types of lichens include rock lichens and sand lichens. A common form of sand lichen is known as reindeer lichen *(Cladonia* spp.)* and is a regular food source for caribou. Lichens are a good environmental indicator, as they do not grow in heavily polluted areas.

Food

Although some species are edible—including old man whisker, black tree lichen and rock tripe—most lichens cannot be eaten because they contain bitter acids and complex carbohydrates that are not easily digested. Be sure that you have identified and selected an edible species. Even edible species are best if boiled first, as they may otherwise cause stomach cramps. Some species make a valuable survival food source; they do not have much flavour, but many are loaded with nutritious proteins, vitamins and minerals. Boiled lichens can be dried and ground into a powder or flour. In Europe, this flour is used to thicken soups, stews, puddings, breads, porridges and sea biscuits. The flour apparently preserves well.

WARNING: Handling lichens on a regular basis can instigate a skin irritation known as woodsman's eczema, which is caused by high amounts of usnic acid found in lichens. When preparing edible species, it is best to soak them in water first and change the water before boiling.

On John Franklin's first expedition, he journeyed through the interior of Canada to the polar seas. When the expedition got into the arctic zone, he and his crew of 6 men ran out of provisions. With food scarce, they managed to survive on tripe lichen, which they found growing on the rocks. All the men survived. On his second expedition, they came by sea through the Bering Strait, well supplied with canned food. As a result of the unfortunate method of sealing cans with lead solder at the time, the food became contaminated. John Franklin and his men eventually became stranded in the ice and ate the contaminated food. No one survived this second voyage.

Green speckleback lichen on a birch tree

Lichen Salad

3 tbsp. (45 mL) black vinegar
3 tbsp. (45 mL) light soy sauce
1 tbsp. (15 mL) packed brown sugar
1 1/2" (3.8 cm) piece of ginger root, finely sliced
3 garlic cloves, diced
1/2 tsp. (2 mL) dried chili flakes
1 tsp. (5 mL) sesame oil
2 spring onions, sliced
2 cups (500 mL) edible lichen
1/2 cup (125 mL) roughly chopped coriander

To prepare the dressing, combine vinegar, soy sauce and brown sugar in a large bowl. Stir until sugar dissolves. Add ginger root, garlic, chili flakes and sesame oil, and stir well. Stir in spring onion. Set aside for 10 minutes. Add lichen and coriander and toss to combine. Transfer to a platter to serve. Makes 5 servings.

Icelandic Lichen Flatbread

Icelandic moss (Cetraria islandica) has the outward appearance of a moss but is a lichen. One cup (250 mL) of soaked Iceland moss is equivalent to about 2 cups (500 mL) of dried material.

2 cups (500 mL) dried Icelandic moss
1 1/2 cup (375 mL) rye flour
1/2 cup (125 mL) stone-ground whole wheat flour
Salt, to taste
1 cup (250 mL) boiling water

Soak Icelandic moss for a few minutes in lukewarm water to soften it. Drain and chop. Combine with rye flour, wheat flour and salt in a large bowl. Gradually add boiling water and stir well, until you have stiff, but pliable dough. Divide dough into 12 equal pieces, roll them out thinly and cut into round flatbreads 18 to 20 cm (7 to 8") in diameter. Prick each flatbread with a fork. Wipe grill with cooking oil and cook flatbreads over high heat until black spots appear, about 2 minutes. Flip flatbread over and cook other side for about 2 minutes. Store flatbreads in a damp cloth or plastic bag, as they dry out quickly. Makes 8 flatbreads.

Sphagnum moss

Moss

Sphagnum riparium and others

Moss grows in moist areas and around detritus such as rotting logs. A perennial evergreen, moss is low-growing and often trails along the ground, with upright leaves that resemble a brush. Leaves reach 5 to 30 cm (2 to 12") in height.

Medicine

Used first by Indigenous peoples, sphagnum moss was also employed as a field dressing during both World Wars to control infections and staunch bleeding. Tea was made to use as a wash on skin irritation such as rash, eczema.

Other Uses

Indigenous peoples used moss to line the interior of moss baskets they used to carry their babies. The moss insulated the babies from the cold and was truly a natural, disposable diaper. Apparently, these babies never got diaper rash, perhaps in part because of the natural iodine in the moss. Sphagnum moss in particular can be used a water purifier because the moss has natural iodine and filtering properties.

153

Poisonous Plants-Common

While many useful and nutritious plants surround us, **it is important to understand potential hazards when dealing with plants.** Many common plants contain irritants and toxins that can seriously harm or cause fatality. Be certain of what you are stalking, as it might end up having the last bite. This chapter outlines a selection of common poisonous plants.

Skunk Cabbage

Symplocarpus foetidus

This low-growing plant grows in swamps and springs, along riverbanks and sometimes as a weed in disturbed mesic areas, yards and gardens. It is a foul-smelling plant characterized by bright yellow, partially rolled flowers, which develop before the broad leaves start to grow.

Skunk cabbage is mildly narcotic and was once used in folk medicine as an expectorant, antispasmodic and diuretic. An overdose can be fatal.

Wild Lettuce

Lactuca virosa,
Syn: *L. seriola*

Also called: lobed prickly lettuce, opium lettuce

This member of the aster family is toxic and is an introduced weed found in alleys, empty lots, gardens, roadsides, disturbed areas and dry, rocky soils. It grows to a height of 2 m (7'). This plant has numerous small, yellow, dandelion-like flowers. Its lower leaves are 5 to 20 cm (2 to 8") long and deeply lobed, whereas its upper leaves clasp the stem. Prickles grow on the underside mid-rib of the leaf. Wild lettuce produces a toxic, milky sap.

Settlers used this plant as a sedative and as a narcotic for pain. This species is listed as a noxious weed in Saskatchewan according to the provincial *Weed Control Act.* In Manitoba, the plant is listed as a Designated Tier 3 noxious weed, but the plant is not listed in Alberta as a prohibited or noxious weed.

Baneberry

Actaea rubra
• *A. pachypoda*

Also called: doll's eye

Baneberry is a member of the buttercup family (Ranunculaceae). It can be found in shady, moist wooded areas in North America. The plant grows to a height of 30 cm (1'). Baneberry leaves are composed of toothed leaflets forming upright clusters. The flower forms along a terminal stalk with a cluster of small whitish to light green flowers. The fruits ripen into shiny red or white berries.

The berries and roots are highly toxic, but all parts of the plant are poisonous. The plant contains protoanemonin and other unknown chemicals. The toxins can have an immediate sedative effect on the cardiac muscle tissue, possibly leading to cardiac arrest if introduced into the bloodstream. If ingested, the berries cause severe symptoms such as nausea, dizziness, headache, increased pulse, acute stomach cramps and gastrointestinal discomfort. For young children, 2 berries could be fatal. For a healthy adult, 6 berries will cause poisoning. Indigenous peoples used the juice from the fruits of various baneberry species to make poison arrow tips.

Immature baneberry

Senega

Polygala senega

Also called: Seneca snakeroot

This member of the milkwort family is toxic. It is found in prairies and parkland meadows, and often in previously disturbed, calcareous soil near aspen bluffs or on roadsides. This low-growing plant has small, pink or greenish-white flowers arranged in a racemose spike and numerous, narrow leaves on the stems.

Traditionally used as a snakebite remedy, senega is now mostly used for respiratory ailments. Toxicity is a result of the saponins in the root. More than a small dose is poisonous.

Black nightshade, pulled from my garden

Black Nightshade

Solanum nigrum

This common plant is a member of the potato family and can be deadly. The plant has a low-growing, spreading habit with oval-shaped leaves pointed at the apex. White or pale pink flowers yield green fruit that ripens to black berries about 6 mm (1/4") across. Introduced to North America, this species is now a common weed. It grows in wastelands and cultivated areas such as gardens.

Nightshade contains an alkaloid called solanine and was once used as an analgesic and sedative. Treat this plant as very poisonous.

Jimsonweed

Datura stramonium

Also called: thorn apple

This member of the potato family is deadly. It is an annual weed that grows in wastelands. This plant grows from about 30 cm to 1 m (1 to 3') to in height and has pointed oval-shaped leaves that are coarse and irregularly toothed. White or purplish, funnel-shaped flowers are present from July to October and produce spiny fruit 3 to 5 cm (1 1/4 to 2") long.

All parts of this plant are extremely poisonous, especially the small, kidney-shaped seeds (20 seeds can kill a small child). Ironically, the plant contains tropane alkaloids, including atropine, used as an antidote for certain poisonings.

Potato

Solanum tuberosum

A member of the potato or nightshade family, the common potato also contains the compound solanine, which is highly toxic if taken in concentrated doses. Solanine collects in the sprouts and in the layer just under the skin of the tuber. Exposure to sunlight during the growth cycle can turn the tubers green. Raw consumption in large quantities of these green tubers can be lethal. The agricultural practice of "hilling" potatoes (piling up soil around each individual plant) helps to control this problem. I often use grass clippings to "hill" my potatoes.

The aerial fruiting body of the plant, which resembles a small green tomato and contains seeds, is also poisonous. When the potato first arrived in Europe, some people did not know which part of the plant to use. The aerial part was inadvertently consumed and poisoning resulted. As a result, it took a while for the potato to become an accepted crop in Europe.

Water Hemlock

Cicuta maculata

This member of the parsley family is deadly and is commonly found along riverbanks, marshlands and swampy, damp areas. It grows 50 cm to 2 m (20" to 7') in height from a stout, magenta-streaked stem with narrow, sharply toothed leaves. Hemlock blooms from June to September with white, umbrella-shaped clusters of small flowers resembling common dill.

The entire plant is poisonous, especially the root. Ingesting small quantities can lead to delirium, vomiting, cramping, severe convulsions and respiratory system failure, followed by a rapid death. Hemlock contains a highly poisonous alkaloid known as coniine. Related plants include dill, wild carrots, cow parsnip (which has a similar flower structure with large leaves and is non-poisonous) and Queen Anne Lace, which can cause skin rashes.

Water hemlock flower

Leaves of water hemlock

Crown Vetch

Coronilla varia

This deadly member of the pea family typically grows in lime-rich soils, grassy areas, parks, hedges, roadsides and wastelands, and can reach a height of 38 cm (15"). The leaves are pinnate, and flowering occurs from June to August. All parts of the plant are highly toxic.

Symptoms of poisoning include diarrhea, severe muscular spasms, coma and death. Once used as a cardio tonic in homeopathy, crown vetch contains a toxic glycoside.

Yellow Sweet Clover

Melilotus officinalis

This member of the pea family is toxic. Yellow sweet clover was introduced as a forage plant and is now a common invasive field plant frequently found in wastelands and on roadsides and embankments. This biennial herb grows from 40 cm to 2.5 m (16" to 8') in height. It has ovoid-shaped fruit pods and yellow flower spikes. Its oval, toothed leaflets are grouped in 3s. Some related varieties in this genus have white flowers and are also toxic.

All parts of this plant are slightly poisonous. As a result of the presence of active principles, including coumarin glycosides, tannins and essential oils, yellow sweet clover has medicinal uses, mostly in ointments and poultices. Symptoms of an overdose include headaches, dizziness, bleeding and vomiting.

Poisonous Plants-
Ornamentals

Many ornamentals found in flower gardens and yards are also poisonous. Belying their pretty appearance, several are deadly. The following is a selection of common poisonous ornamentals. I found many of these plants in my yard shortly after moving in. The house was built in the 1940s in an older area in Saskatoon, and the large yard contained several pockets of beautiful ornamentals, probably planted at least a generation before my family moved in.

Indian Turnip

Arisaema triphyllum

Also called: dragon turnip, Jack-in-the-pulpit, wild pepper

This member of the arum family is toxic. Indigenous to eastern North America, this plant has been introduced into western Canada as a decorative bedding cultivar. Suited for moist, shady areas, it grows from 30 cm to 1 m (1 to 3') tall. The plant is characterized by purple and green striping, an unusual upper leaf-like spathe folded over as a hood to shade the tube-like flowering portion, trifoliate (3 leaflet) leaf clusters and small clusters of red berries.

The root was once a traditional food source and may be edible if properly prepared through cooking and/or extensive drying. The plant contains acrid calcium oxalate crystals that, if the plant is eaten without proper preparation, can intensely irritate the mouth and mucous membranes.

Garden Rhubarb

Rheum rhabarbarum

Rhubarb is a member of the buckwheat family and has been introduced as a food plant. It has large palmately shaped leaves and thick, tuberous roots and can grow 1 m (3') or more in height. The edible portion of the rhubarb is the petiole stalk (stem).

The leaves are poisonous and contain several anthro-glycosides that can cause fatal poisonings. Milder reactions to the toxins can result in kidney disorders. The leaves can be used to control low-growing weeds by laying the leaves over top.

Field Larkspur

Delphinium consolida, Syn: *Consolida regalis*

Also called: forking larkspur

This member of the buttercup family is highly poisonous. Larkspur is a small to large flowering plant reaching about 30 to 80 cm (12 to 32") tall. Originally native to the Mediterranean region, this plant is now globally distributed. The plant is erect and characterized by 5-petalled bluish flowers that have an upward-curving spur. Flowers occur in a loose terminal inflorescence from June until August. This plant can be identified early in its lifecycle by its finely divided leaves, which alternate on the stem. It is frequently grown as a cultivar and is often found in gardens and in wastelands.

Except for the flowers, all parts of this plant are poisonous, especially the flattened black seeds. Larkspur is frequently used for decorative purposes but is also used as an insecticide for lice and nits. Alkaloids within the plant can cause weakness and respiratory failure.

WARNING: Before flowering, the immature plant resembles dill in its early stages, so be careful if both species grow in your yard.

Monkshood

Aconitum napellus

This deadly member of the buttercup family was introduced to North America as a decorative cultivar. It is a tall perennial herb, reaching a height of 1.5 m (5'), with an erect stem and alternate, palmately divided leaves. It has a tuberous root and hooded violet, blue or yellow flowers arranged in tall terminal spikes. The plant is known to have escaped cultivation in some areas of the prairies .

All parts of the monkshood plant are deadly poisonous, and any contact with the plant can be dangerous. The plant contains alkaloids including aconitine, one of the most potent nerve poisons in the plant kingdom.

Iris • Flag Iris • Garden Iris

Iris germanica • I. pseudacorus • I. versicolor • I. florentina

These and other members of the iris family are poisonous. Introduced to North America, these perennial plants have a creeping rhizome bearing stiff sword-shaped greyish-green leaves and a tall stem 10 to 80 cm (4 to 32") in height, topped with large, showy, blue-violet, occasionally yellow or white, fragrant flowers.

The leaves, and especially the roots, are poisonous and can cause vomiting and nausea.

Ivy

Hedera helix

This evergreen woody vine, native to Europe and Asia, is frequently cultivated in North America as a house and yard plant and is poisonous. Its dark-green, alternate leaves are leathery and shiny, often with pale venation. Leaves on the non-flowering stem are usually cordate (heart) shaped and pointed away from the stem; flowering stem leaves are palmate, with 3 to 5 lobes. The flowers themselves grow in small, greenish-yellow terminal umbels and produce small blue-black berry-like drupes, similar to tiny plums.

Young ivy leaves have medicinal uses for certain cardiac and respiratory problems, and are also used as an expectorant and antispasmodic. Large doses cause vessel constriction and can slow the heart rate dangerously. If eaten, the berries mainly have a purgative effect, but more severe symptoms can occur if large quantities are consumed. The berries and growth form of the plant loosely resemble wild grape, so be careful if both ivy and grape grow in your yard.

Lily-of-the-Valley

Convallaria majalis, Syn: *Maianthemum canadense*

Also called: two-leaved Solomon's seal

This member of the lily family is extremely poisonous. It is a low-growing undergrowth plant found in moist shaded areas throughout the Prairies. A common ornamental, it frequently grows in dense bunches, 5 to 15 cm (2 to 6") high, usually with 2 or 3 ovate leaves alternating on the stem. The flowers are small and white, and they cluster in a raceme. The fruit is composed of red berries approximately 6 mm (1/4") in diameter. All parts of this plant are extremely poisonous. Children should be warned not to consume the berries, as they can cause paralysis and respiratory failure if medical attention is not promptly sought. The plant contains cardiac glycosides, which are used in heart medications.

Peony

Paeonia officinalis

This poisonous species was introduced as a decorative garden plant from southeastern Europe. The plant grows to the height of 60 to 70 cm (24 to 28"). It has tuberous roots and a stout erect, branched stem with large reddish or white showy flowers characterized by 8 outside petals and numerous smaller inner petals. The fruiting body forms a capsule, which holds shiny, black seeds.

All parts of this plant are poisonous, especially the flowers. Active constituents include glycosides, peregrinine (an alkaloid) and an anthocyanidin pigment (paeonidin) that gives the plant antispasmodic, diuretic, vasoconstrictive and sedative properties. Various herbalists use peonies as an ingredient in Chinese medicine.

Bird-in-the-Bush

Corydalis cava, Syn: *C. bulbosa*

Also called: bulbous corydalis

This member of the poppy family is poisonous. The plant is an erect perennial herb that grows 15 to 30 cm (6 to 12") tall and is characterized by 2 deeply lobed, alternate compound leaves that are blue-green below and light green above. The irregularly shaped violet or white flowers form a terminal spike-like raceme. Individual flowers have a pronounced long, curved spur. The root system is composed of a single bulbous underground tuber with wiry roots.

Tubers are used medicinally; powerful alkaloids within the roots have antispasmodic, sedative and blood-pressure-lowering properties appropriate for treating neurological diseases such as Parkinson's disease. Large doses can cause severe headaches and other serious side effects.

Iranian Poppy

Papaver bracteatum

This member of the poppy family is also poisonous. This poppy is a perennial herb characterized by a covering of white hairs. It has a branched taproot and develops a basal rosette of pinnately divided, toothed leaves during the first year of growth. The plant can reach a height of 20 cm (8"). Subsequent yearly growth produces tall, red solitary flowers with leafy bracts immediately beneath the flowers; these bracts distinguish this species from the opium poppy, which has no such bracts.

All parts of the plant are poisonous. The roots are used medicinally, especially in the production of codeine.

Opium Poppy

Papaver somniferum

This member of the poppy family is very poisonous. Introduced to North America, this annual plant is usually found growing as an ornamental in gardens, though it has occasionally escaped and become established in the wild. The plant is usually 60 cm to 1 m (2 to 3') in height with a slightly hairy stem, glossy blue-green leaves and a roundish fruit capsule. Its solitary flower is about 5 to 10 cm (2 to 4") across and can be white, purple, orange or red depending on the variety.

All parts of the plant exude latex and are extremely poisonous, with the exception of the ripe seeds. Potent alkaloids found in the plant include morphine and codeine. Extracts, mostly from the plant latex, are used in medicine as an analgesic and anti-spasmodic. Long-term use and misuse can cause addiction to narcotic opiates, general deterioration and death.

Yellow Water Lily • White Water Lily

Nuphar lutea • *Nymphaea alba*

These members of the water lily family are toxic. These perennial aquatic herbs are native to Europe and Asia and are sometimes found in aquatic gardens. They have long-stalked, floating, leathery, ovate- to cordate-shaped leaves with either yellow or showy white flowers.

The rhizomes on both plants contain constituents used in medicine for their cardiotonic and other properties. Large amounts of the yellow water lily can result in paralysis, and the white water lily is considered to be similarly dangerous.

Wood Sorrel

Oxalis acetosella

This common houseplant is originally from woodland areas of Europe. The plant grows about 15 cm (6") in height. Long-stalked, trifoliate leaves are clover-like and droop along the midrib during nights of bad weather. Flowers are usually white with violet veins, although purple variations sometimes occur.

The aerial parts of this plant contain potassium oxalate and oxalic acid, which are irritants that can cause haemorrhaging, diarrhoea and kidney failure.

Attracting Birds
and Pollinators

Spaces in the yard or balcony can be places of rejuvenation and revitalization—not just for us, but also for wildlife.

Birds play an important role in creating and maintaining bio-diversity. For instance, they move seed about, sometimes to great distances, and thus provide mobility for plants to move and adapt. They also help create peaceful space with their song and activity, and help keep the bugs down in the summer. Planting a few shrubs or trees is an easy way to create habitat for birds. Other plants, such as flowers, will also attract birds, butterflies and bees. All that is required to entice birds to your yard is a secure environment suitable for nesting or feeding, clean water nearby and a variety of bugs and seeds for food. Well-placed birdhouses will most likely attract birds into the area. Birdhouses are built with different sized entrance holes, so do a little research to determine what hole size different species require to determine what size you need to attract various species. Leaf compost will provide a home for many varieties of bugs that birds will enjoy and also provides an excellent media for growing potatoes.

Wildlife and plants are inextricably bound together in a vital web of life support. The importance of this web is especially evident when looking at the relationships between pollinators and plants, upon which humankind has become precariously dependent. Bees make approximately 15 to 30 percent of the world's food supply possible. Bees are the premier pollinators of the world and without them farmers and gardeners globally might experience massive crop failures. Bees need flowers for both nectar and pollen, nectar being an energy source that honeybees use to

make honey, while pollen is protein-rich food. According to a 2004 National Geographic News article, honeybee numbers have declined by nearly 50 percent in the last 50 years. Although parasites and disease are partly to blame, many other factors, such as habitat modification and exposure to chemicals, contribute to the decline in bee populations. Other yet unknown, complex and cumulative factors may also be at work.

This decline appears to be slowing down somewhat and even improving slightly in the United States; however, bee populations still appear to be a long way from recovery there. In Alberta, commercial bee colonies appear to be on the mend as a result of improved organic methods for management of bee colonies (CBC News, 2017).

Butterflies are also key pollinators. They favour broad flower heads rich in nectar as a food source and are essential for transferring pollen to other flowers. I have grown showy milkweed in my yard for many years and have enjoyed one season of rare monarch butterflies thus far. While the butterflies were present, I did not harvest any milkweed, choosing instead to leave the plants undisturbed as long as the butterflies were using them. The milkweeds continue to flourish, and I am awaiting the monarchs' return. The monarch is a federally protected species under the *Species at Risk Act*.

We can help these pollinators in our own space. Decreasing the use of pesticides is one way to protect these creatures. Creating safe habitats is another valuable way to help, such as by maintaining a variety of plants that bloom during the spring, summer and early autumn seasons. Pollinator gardens also need water. Scavenging rainwater runoff, such as from the eaves, provides a cheap, clean source of water that can also reduce municipal water demand. An area of wet sand will attract both bees and butterflies and is both safer and more suitable than ponds, as ponds and bird baths may be too deep for the insects.

Echinacea purpurea

Suggested flowers for attracting butterflies, bees and birds:

NATIVE AND INTRODUCED PLANTS:

Bee Balm, Bergamot, *Monarda* spp.

Sunflowers, *Helianthus* spp.

Blazing Star, *Liatris* spp.

Purple Coneflower, *Echinacea purpurea*

Black-eyed Susan, *Rudbeckia fulgida*

Goldenrod, *Solidago* spp.

Milkweed, *Asclepias* spp.,
Dwarfed Milkweed, *Asclepias tuberose*

Purple Prairie Clover, *Dalea purpurea*

Fireweed, *Epilobium angustifolium*

CULTIVARS:

Basil, *Ocimum basilicum*

Thyme, *Thymus* spp.

Oregano, *Origanum* spp.

Lavender, *Lavandula* spp.

Chives, *Allium schoenoprasum*

Glossary

Achene: a small, dry, one-seeded nut-like fruit that does not split open to release the seed.

Anther: the part of a stamen that holds pollen.

Catkin: a linear cluster of small flowers, usually of one sex, with inconspicuous or no petals, surrounded by downy bracts.

Cladode: a leaf-like stem that is flattened or scale like.

Corolla: the petals of a flower considered collectively.

Cyme: a cluster of flowers that blooms first at the tip of the main branch, with subsequent flowers blooming on terminal buds of lateral stems.

Dioecious: a plant that has the male and female reproductive organs in separate individuals.

Flora: a book or work describing the plants considered as a group, especially the plants of a particular region or time, often with the goal of identification.

Inflorescence: the complete flowering portion of a plant including stems, stalks, bracts and flowers.

Lanceolate: lance shaped, usually long and narrow, or much longer than wide, tapering to a point at one or both ends.

Monoecious: a plant that has both male and female reproductive organs on the same plant, but in different flowers.

Ovate: shaped like an egg, usually with the broad end toward the base.

Palmately lobed: a leaf that is divided into 3 or more distinct lobes, like a hand with outstretched fingers.

Petiole: a leaf stalk.

Pistil: the female reproductive parts of a flower, where it will produce seeds.

Propagules: the fruiting body or portion of a plant that can become detached from a plant and give rise to a new plant.

Racemose spike: an unbranched, indeterminate and elongated inflorescence with flowers that do not have a pedicels or short flower stalks. Younger flowers develop towards the growing end or tip, while the older flowers mature at the base of the spike.

Sepal: one of the outermost, usually green parts of a flower that surrounds and protects the flower petals and bud, typically extending from the base of a flower after it has opened.

Stamen: the male reproductive organ of the flower, which produces pollen.

Stolons: often called runners, stolons are stems that grow along the surface of the soil or just below ground, forming roots at the nodes and new plants at the buds.

Style: the stalk or middle part of the female reproductive organ in a plant, connecting the stigma and ovary.

Tepal: a flower part having no differentiation between petals and sepals.

Umbel globular: often a flat-topped flower cluster where the flower stalks come from a common point, much like an umbrella.

References

Anderson, Stanley F. and Raymond. Hull. *The Art Of Making Wine*. Don Mills: Longman Canada Limited, 1974.

Best of Bridge. *The Best of the Best and More*. Calgary: Best of Bridge Publishing Limited, 1998.

Bruggen, Theodore V. *Wildflowers Grasses & Other Plants of the Northern Plains and Black Hills*. South Dakota: Badlands Natural History Association, 1992.

Bunney, Sarah, ed. *The Illustrated Encyclopaedia of Herbs: Their Medicinal and Culinary Uses*. Toronto: Chancellor Press, 1993.

Carmichael, Lloyd T. *Prairie Wildflowers*. Toronto: J.M. Dent & Son Canada Limited, 1961.

Chambers, F. H. and A. Karst. *Wild Berries of Alberta, Saskatchewan and Manitoba*. Edmonton: Lone Pine Publishing, 2012.

Diamond, Jared. *Guns, Germs, and Steel: The Fates of Human Societies*. New York: W. W. Norton & Company, 1997.

Elliot, D. *Wild Roots: A Forage's Guide to the Edible and Medicinal Roots, Tubers Corms, and Rhizomes of North America*. Rochester: Healing Arts Press, 1995.

Flax Council of Canada. *Family Favourites Flax: Recipes and "Healthful" Tips*. Winnipeg, MB: Flax Council of Canada, 2009.

Franklin, J. *Narrative of a Journey to the Shores of the Polar Sea In the Years 1819-20-21-22*. London: J.M. Dent & Sons Ltd., 1909.

Frankton, Clarence and Gerald Mulligan. *Weeds of Canada*. Toronto: NC Press Limited in Cooperation with Agriculture Canada and the Canadian Government Publishing Centre Supply and Services Canada, 1997.

Gibbons, Euell. *Stalking the Wild Asparagus*. Brattleboro: Alan C Hood & Company, Inc., 1962.

Hale, Mason. *How to Know the Lichens*. Dubuque: Wm. C. Brown Company Publishers, 1944.

Hutchens, Alma. *A Handbook of Native American Herbs*. Boston: Shambhala, 1992.

Johnson, D., L. Kershaw, A. Mackinnon and J. Pojar. *Plants of the Western Boreal Forest & Aspen Parkland*. Edmonton: Lone Pine Publishing, 1995.

Kershaw, Linda. *Edible & Medicinal Plants of the Rockies*. Edmonton: Lone Pine Publishing, 2000.

Kershaw, Linda. *Saskatchewan Wayside Wildflowers*. Edmonton: Lone Pine Publishing, 2003.

Kindscher, K. *Edible Wild Plants of the Prairie: An Ethnobotanical Guide*. Lawrence, KA: University Press of Kansas, 1987.

Kochanski, Mors. *Bushcraft: Outdoor Skills and Wilderness Survival*. Edmonton: Lone Pine Publishing, 1987.

Laws, Bill. *Fifty Plants that Changed the Course of History*. Buffalo: Firefly Books. (U.S.) Inc., 2010.

Looman, J., and K.F. Best. *Budd's Flora of the Canadian Prairie Provinces*. Publication 1662. Ottawa: Research Branch, Agriculture Canada, 1979.

Mabey, Richard. *Food for Free*. London: HarperCollins Publishers, 2004.

Mackinnon, A., L. Kershaw, J. Arnason, P. Owen, A. Karst, and F.H. Chambers. *Edible & Medicinal Plants of Canada*. Edmonton: Lone Pine Publishing, 2014.

Marles, R. J., C. Clavelle, L. Monteleone, N. Tays, D. Burns. 2000. *Aboriginal Plant Use in Canada's Northwest Boreal Forest.* Vancouver: UBC Press, 2000.

Medsger, Oliver P. *Edible Wild Plants.* New York: Collier-Macmillan Publishers, 1966.

Meehan, Joe. *Common Saskatchewan River Valley Plants.* Battleford, SK: Marian Press Ltd., 1995.

Métis Cookbook and Guide to Healthy Living. 2nd ed. Ottawa: National Aboriginal Health Organization, 2008.

Moss, E.H. *Flora of Alberta.* 2nd ed. Revised by J.G. Packer. Toronto: University of Toronto Press, 1996.

Peterson, Lee A. *A Field Guide to Edible Wild Plants: Eastern and Central North America.* Boston: Houghton Mifflin Company, 1977.

Prescott, G. W. *How to Know the Aquatic Plants.* Dubuque: Wm. C. Brown Company Publishers, 1944.

Ramsay, Gordon. *In the Heat of the Kitchen.* London: Quadrille Publishing Limited, 2003.

Savage, Candace. *Prairie: A Natural History.* Vancouver: Greystone Books, 2004.

Schofield, J. J. *Discovering Wild Plants: Alaska, Western Canada, the Northwest.* Bothell, WA: Alaska Northwest Books, 1989.

Schauenberg, P., and F. Paris. *Guide to Medicinal Plants.* New Canaan, CT.: Keats, 1977.

Snell, Alma. *A Taste Of Heritage: Crow Indian Recipes and Herbal Medicnes.* Lincoln: University of Nebraska Press, 2006.

Stark, R. *Guide to Indian Herbs.* Surrey: Hancock House, 1992.

Szczawinski, Adam, and Nancy Turner. *Edible Garden Weeds of Canada.* Canada's Edible Wild Plants Series Vol. 1. Markham: National Museum of Natural Sciences, 1988.

Szczawinski, Adam, and Nancy Turner. *Wild Green Vegetables of Canada.* Edible Wild Plants of Canada. No. 4. Ottawa: National Museum of Natural Sciences, 1980.

Tilford, Gregory L. *Edible and Medicinal Plants of the West.* Missoula: Mountain Press Publishing Company, 1997.

Turner, Nancy. *The Earth's Blanket.* Vancouver: Douglas & McIntyre, 2005.

Turner, Nancy, and Adam Szczawinski. *Common Poisonous Plants and Mushrooms Of North America.* Portland: Timber Press, 1991.

Turner, Nancy, and Adam Szczawinski. *Wild Coffee and Tea Substitutes of Canada.* Edible Wild Plants of Canada No. 2. Ottawa: National Museum of Natural Sciences, 1978.

Turner, Nancy, and Adam Szczawinski. *Edible Wild Fruits and Nuts of Canada.* Canada's Edible Wild Plants Series, Vol. 3. Markham: National Museum of Canada, 1988.

Vance, F.R., J. R. Jowsey, J. S. McLean, F. A. Switzer. *Wildflowers Across the Prairies.* Vancouver: Greystone Books, 1999.

Vance, R. F., J. R. Jowsey, J. S. McLean. *Wildflowers Across the Prairies, Revised and Expanded.* Saskatoon, Saskatchewan. Western Producer Prairie Books, 1984.

Weatherford, Jack. *Indian Givers: How Native Americans Transformed the World.* New York: Three Rivers Press, 2010.

Whitecap Books. *The Essential Asian Cook Book.* Vancouver. Whitecap Books, 1997.

Internet References

Alberta Parks. "Online Tracking and Watch Lists." Last modified November 3, 2017. https://www.albertaparks.ca/albertaparksca/management-land-use/alberta-conservation-information-management-system-acims/tracking-watch-lists/.

Alberta Queen's Printer. "Weed Control Act, Weed Control Regulation. Alberta Regulation 19/2010. With Amendments up to and including Alberta Regulation 125/2016." http://www.qp.alberta.ca/documents/Regs/2010_019.pdf.

Big Oven. "Anise Hyssop Sauce for Roast Lamb." Accessed January 2014. http://www.bigoven.com/recipe/19547/anise-hyssop-sauce-for-roast-lamb.

CBC News. "Alberta Bees Bounce Back as Monitoring Leads to Healthier Hives." Last modified August 9, 2017. http://www.cbc.ca/news/canada/edmonton/bees-alberta-colonies-mites-1.4239706.

Global Cookbook. "Gooseberry Bergamot Jelly Recipe." Accessed January 2012. https://cookeatshare.com/recipes/gooseberry-bergamot-jelly-191821.

Government of Canada. "Species at Risk Public Registry." Accessed January 2018. https://www.registrelep-sararegistry.gc.ca/species/speciesDetails_e.cfm?sid=294.

Manitoba Agriculture. "Declaration of Noxious Weeds in Manitoba." Accessed January 2018. https://www.gov.mb.ca/agriculture/crops/weeds/declaration-of-noxious-weeds-in-mb.html.

Manitoba Conservation Data Centre. "Species and Plant Communities." Accessed January 2018. https://www.gov.mb.ca/sd/cdc/db.html.

Manitoba Pork. "Maple Glazed Rack of Pork Recipe." Accessed January 2012. http://manitobapork.com/recipe/maple-glazed-manitoba-rack-of-pork/.

Penn University Archives and Records Centre. "John William Harshberger Papers 1886 to 1929." Last modified August 2017. http://www.archives.upenn.edu/faids/upt/upt50/harshberger_jw.html

Roach, John. "Bee Decline May Spell End of Some Fruits, Vegetables." National Geographic News, October 5, 2017. http://news.nationalgeographic.com/news/2004/10/1005_041005_honeybees.html.

Saskatchewan Conservation Data Centre. "Species Lists." Accessed January 2018. http://www.biodiversity.sk.ca/spplist.htm.

Saskatchewan Minister of Agriculture. "The Weed Control Act." Last modified 2010. http://publications.gov.sk.ca/documents/20/84083-44fb5d3e-a7e0-461c-84d5-876f651a3ed4.pdf.

University of Wisconsin. "The UWGB Linothorax Project: Reconstructing and Testing Ancient Linen Body Armor." Accessed January 2015. www.uwgb.edu/aldreteg/Linothorax.html

Walker, Sandra. "Lesson Plans for Saskatchewan Native Plant Society, for Schools Grade 1 to 6." Last modified 2012. https://www.npss.sk.ca/docs/2_pdf/Grade_1_Lesson_Plan.pdf to https://www.npss.sk.ca/docs/2_pdf/Grade_6_Lesson_Plan.pdf.

Plant Index

Recipe Index

About the Author

SANDRA WALKER is an accomplished ethnobotanist and educator who has spent her life first learning about wild foods and plants and then teaching others about them. Born in Hamilton, she kindled her interest in wild foods when planting trees in Northern Canada and cooking on a solar stove in the wilderness with her husband. Sandra has worked as an educator in Saskatchewan for major local nature centres, school systems and Indigenous organizations.

She is currently employed as program facilitator, ethnobotanist and archaeologist at Saskatoon's Brightwater Science Environmental and Indigenous Learning Centre. Sandra has a double honours degree in archaeology/Anthropology and fine arts from the University of Saskatchewan. She is a nature columnist and author of several publications and educational plans. She lives with her husband and two adult sons in Saskatoon.